HOW TO BUILD A **ROBOT** (WITH YOUR DAD)

HOW TO BUILD A ROBOT (WITH YOUR DAD)

AUBREY SMITH

FIRST PUBLISHED IN GREAT BRITAIN IN 2012 BY
MICHAEL O'MARA BOOKS LIMITED
9 LION YARD
TREMADOC ROAD
LONDON SW4 7NQ

A CIP CATALOGUE RECORD FOR THIS BOOK IS AVAILABLE FROM THE BRITISH LIBRARY.

PAPERS USED BY MICHAEL O'MARA BOOKS LIMITED ARE NATURAL, RECYCLABLE
PRODUCTS MADE FROM WOOD GROWN IN SUSTAINABLE FORESTS. THE MANUFACTURING
PROCESSES CONFORM TO THE ENVIRONMENTAL REGULATIONS OF THE COUNTRY OF
ORIGIN.

ISBN: 978-1-84317-878-1

1 2 3 4 5 6 7 8 9 10

WWW.MOMBOOKS.COM

PRINTED AND BOUND IN FINLAND BY BOOKWELL

DEDICATED TO
THOMAS, EMILY AND OSCAR – MY FAVOURITE HUMANS

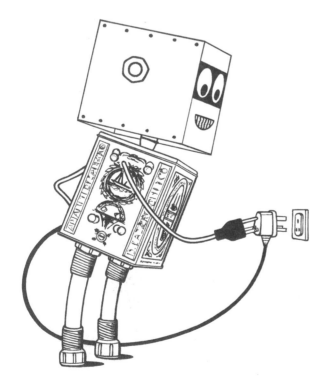

CONTENTS

HELLO HUMANS (AND HUMANS' DADS), MY NAME IS OTTO AND THIS IS MY DAD ZIPPY. WE'VE BEEN PROGRAMMED TO SHOW YOU HOW TO BUILD SOME ROBOTS OF YOUR OWN. THERE ARE TWENTY EASY-TO-BUILD ROBOT PROJECTS IN THIS BOOK AND MOST CAN BE MADE IN AN AFTERNOON, USING THINGS YOU'D USUALLY FIND AROUND YOUR HOUSE.

OUR INSTRUCTIONS ARE REALLY JUST A GUIDE – IF YOU DON'T HAVE EXACTLY WHAT WE USED, USE WHATEVER IS TO HAND. IT'S ALL ABOUT USING YOUR IMAGINATION AND HAVING FUN!

THIS IS A PICTURE OF MY DOG 'SCOOTER'. HE LIKES ENGINE OIL AND HAVING HIS TUMMY POLISHED. BUT MAINLY HE LIKES RUNNING AWAY. SEE HOW MANY TIMES YOU CAN SPOT HIM IN THIS BOOK.

IF YOU SEE HIM SHOUT 'SCOOTER!'

OUR TOOLKIT

STEEL RULE (FOR CUTTING STRAIGHT EDGES)
STRONG TAPE (SUCH AS ELECTRICAL INSULATING TAPE)
PVA GLUE (FOR STICKING PAPER AND CARD)
HI-TACK GLUE (FOR STICKING METAL, PLASTIC ETC.)
PLIERS
WIRE CUTTERS
SCREWDRIVERS
DRILL
AWL (TO MAKE HOLES)
HACKSAW
SCISSORS
CRAFT KNIFE

LOTS OF OUR PROJECTS USE PAPER MACHE. IT'S FUN AND
WILL MAKE YOUR ROBOTS STRONGER AND EASIER TO PAINT.
YOU MAKE IT BY SOAKING NEWSPAPER IN EITHER,
A) WALLPAPER PASTE (BE CAREFUL IF THERE ARE VERY
SMALL HUMANS AROUND – WALLPAPER PASTE IS NOT
GOOD TO EAT!) OR B) WATERED-DOWN PVA GLUE. SIMPLY
DIP LONG STRIPS OF OLD NEWSPAPER INTO A BOWL OF
YOUR CHOSEN GLOOP AND APPLY WITH YOUR FINGERS,
OR A PAINTBRUSH, IN EVEN LAYERS AND LET IT DRY
THOROUGHLY BEFORE PAINTING.

PROJECT 1:
CARDBOARD CLASSIC

THIS IS A REALLY SIMPLE ROBOT MODEL MADE MAINLY FROM PACKAGING SALVAGED FROM THE RECYCLING BOX.

FOR THIS PROJECT YOU WILL NEED: A BOX FOR THE BODY – A LARGE CEREAL OR SOAP POWDER BOX; A SMALLER BOX FOR THE HEAD – A SQUARISH TEA BAG BOX IS IDEAL; TWO MATCHING BOXES FOR ARMS – THE TYPE TOOTHPASTE COMES IN; TWO CRISP TUBES WITH METAL BOTTOMS (MAKE SURE YOU HAVE EATEN ALL THE CRISPS), TWO MATCHING BOXES ABOUT THE SAME SIZE AS THE HEAD FOR FEET, SOME OLD NEWSPAPERS AND PASTE FOR PAPER MACHE, TWO MATCHING SCREWTOPS FROM WATER OR POP BOTTLES, SOME STRONG STICKY TAPE.

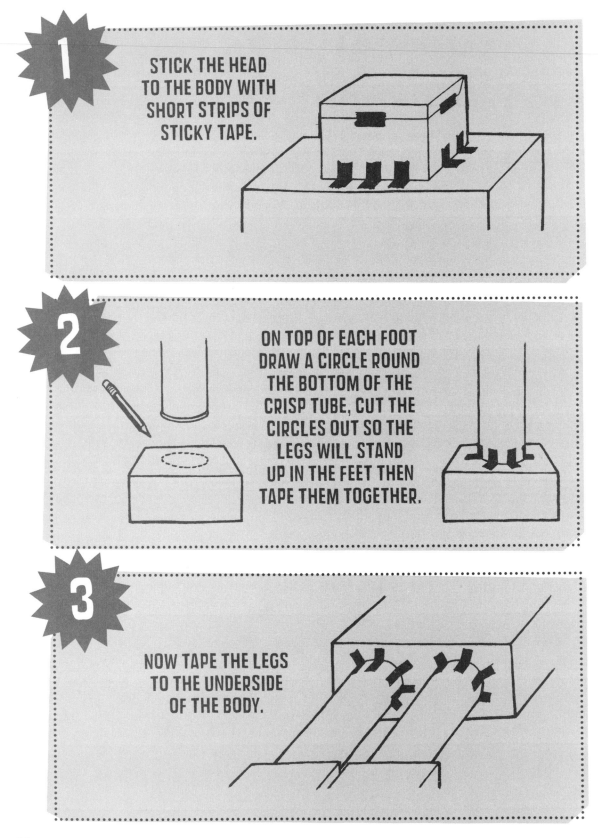

1 STICK THE HEAD TO THE BODY WITH SHORT STRIPS OF STICKY TAPE.

2 ON TOP OF EACH FOOT DRAW A CIRCLE ROUND THE BOTTOM OF THE CRISP TUBE, CUT THE CIRCLES OUT SO THE LEGS WILL STAND UP IN THE FEET THEN TAPE THEM TOGETHER.

3 NOW TAPE THE LEGS TO THE UNDERSIDE OF THE BODY.

4

TAPE ON HIS ARMS. YOU MAY CHOOSE TO HAVE ARMS BY HIS SIDE, STICKING STRAIGHT OUT OR EVEN ONE OF EACH. GLUE ON THE TWO BOTTLE TOPS FOR EYES.

5

COVER YOUR ROBOT WITH PAPER MACHE USING THICKER LAYERS AROUND THE TAPED JOINTS FOR EXTRA STRENGTH. THE PAPER MACHE WILL ALSO MAKE THE ROBOT EASIER TO PAINT.

6

WHEN THE PAPER MACHE IS DRY IT IS READY TO PAINT. WE PAINTED OURS RED (BODY) AND YELLOW (HEAD, ARMS AND LEGS). DETAILS CAN NOW BE ADDED OR PAINTED USING COLOURED CARD OR PAPER SHAPES. NOW GIVE HIM (OR HER!) A NAME.

OUR NEXT PROJECT REQUIRES A HUMAN VOLUNTEER - MEET CHARLIE. LIKE MOST HUMANS, CHARLIE WOULD MUCH RATHER BE A ROBOT. IF YOU WOULD TOO, FOLLOW THESE INSTRUCTIONS AND MAKE YOUR OWN ROBOT COSTUME!

PROJECT 2: ROBOT SUIT

TO BE A WALKING, TALKING ROBOT YOU WILL NEED:

LARGE CARDBOARD BOX
(BIG ENOUGH TO REACH FROM YOUR NECK TO YOUR WAIST)

EXTRA LARGE WATER BOTTLE
(BIGGER THAN YOUR HEAD)

TWO LENGTHS OF VENT-DUCTING
(AS LONG AS YOUR ARMS)

AN OLD HOODIE

WIRE COAT HANGER

SOME STICKY-BACKED VELCRO

SPRAY PAINT (WE RECOMMEND GREY OR SILVER)

VERY STRONG COTTON THREAD AND A NEEDLE

GLUE, PLIERS AND A CRAFT KNIFE

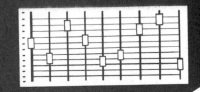

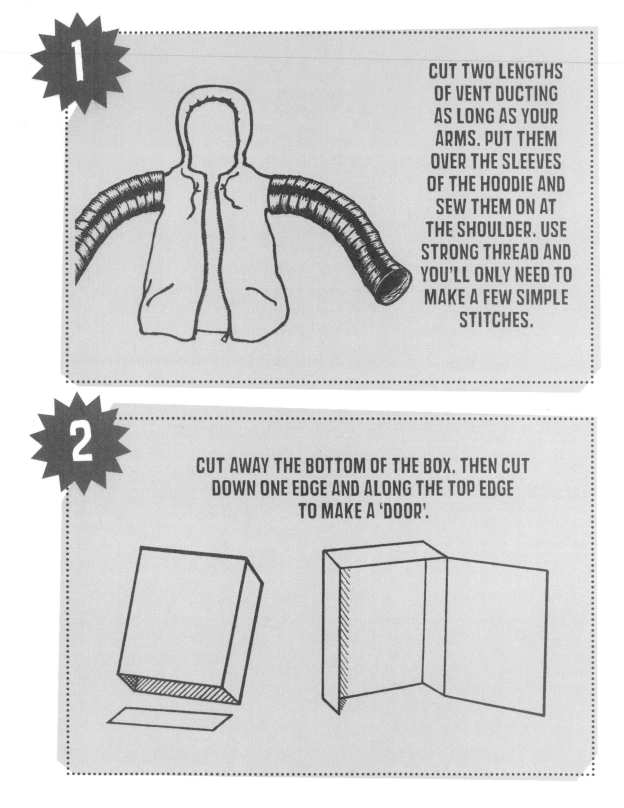

1

CUT TWO LENGTHS OF VENT DUCTING AS LONG AS YOUR ARMS. PUT THEM OVER THE SLEEVES OF THE HOODIE AND SEW THEM ON AT THE SHOULDER. USE STRONG THREAD AND YOU'LL ONLY NEED TO MAKE A FEW SIMPLE STITCHES.

2

CUT AWAY THE BOTTOM OF THE BOX. THEN CUT DOWN ONE EDGE AND ALONG THE TOP EDGE TO MAKE A 'DOOR'.

3

CUT A 'U'-SHAPE OUT OF THE TOP OF THE BOX, BIG ENOUGH TO FIT YOUR NECK INTO (DON'T FORGET YOU'LL HAVE A HOODIE ON). THEN CUT TWO ARM-HOLES IN THE SIDES, BIG ENOUGH FOR THE VENT DUCTING TO GO THROUGH.

4

GLUE TWO STRIPS OF CARDBOARD (WITH A FOLD IN THE CENTRE) TO THE TOP AND BOTTOM OF THE 'DOOR'.

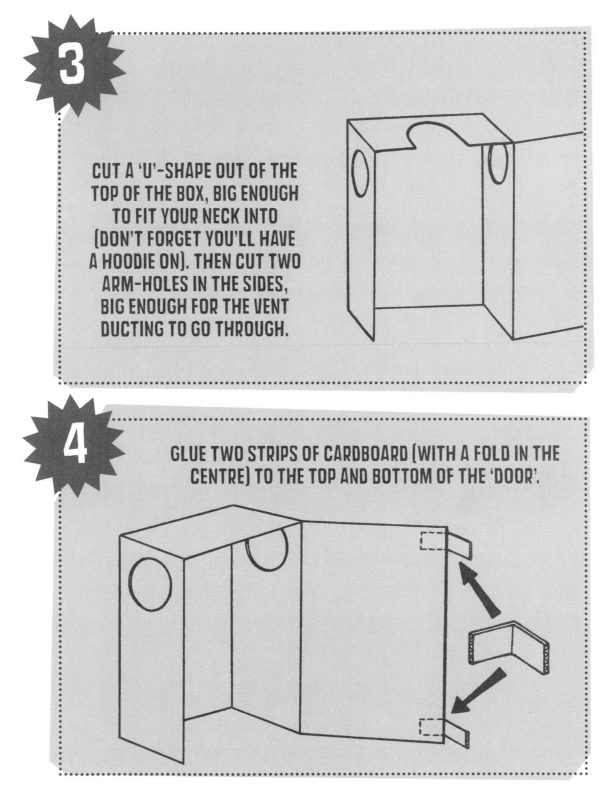

5

ASK YOUR DAD TO CUT AWAY THE BOTTOM PART OF THE BOTTLE, LEAVING A SECTION WHICH WILL FIT COMFORTABLY OVER YOUR HEAD.

6

PUT A BOTTLE ON AND MARK OUT A SMALL RECTANGLE AROUND YOUR EYES. REMOVE THE BOTTLE AND CUT THE SHAPE OUT CAREFULLY. IF THE CUT EDGES FEEL A LITTLE SHARP, RUB THEM DOWN WITH SANDPAPER. THIS GOES FOR THE BOTTOM EDGE TOO.

7

IN THE TWO 'SHOE' BOXES CUT HOLES BIG ENOUGH TO FIT YOUR FEET THROUGH (WITHOUT YOUR SHOES - YOU CAN PUT YOUR SHOES ON ONCE YOUR FEET ARE INSIDE).

8

NOW GET DAD TO DO THE SPRAY PAINTING (THIS IS BEST DONE OUTSIDE). SPRAY THE FOOT BOXES, THE BODY BOX AND THE BOTTLE FOR THE HEAD - REMOVE THE LID FROM THE BOTTLE AND SPRAY IT SEPARATELY.

23

9

WHEN THE PAINT IS COMPLETELY DRY, TAKE THE 'BODY' AND STICK SQUARES OF VELCRO AS SHOWN. THESE ARE TO HOLD THE BACK CLOSED ONCE YOU HAVE THE SUIT ON.

10

BEND THE HOOK OF A WIRE COAT HANGER ROUND THE BASE OF THE SCREW THREAD AND CLAMP IT IN PLACE BY SCREWING ON THE LID. BEND THE HANGER INTO AN UPRIGHT LOOP. YOU MAY NEED TO USE PLIERS.

11

NOW DECORATE THE HEAD AND BODY – HERE'S WHAT WE USED...

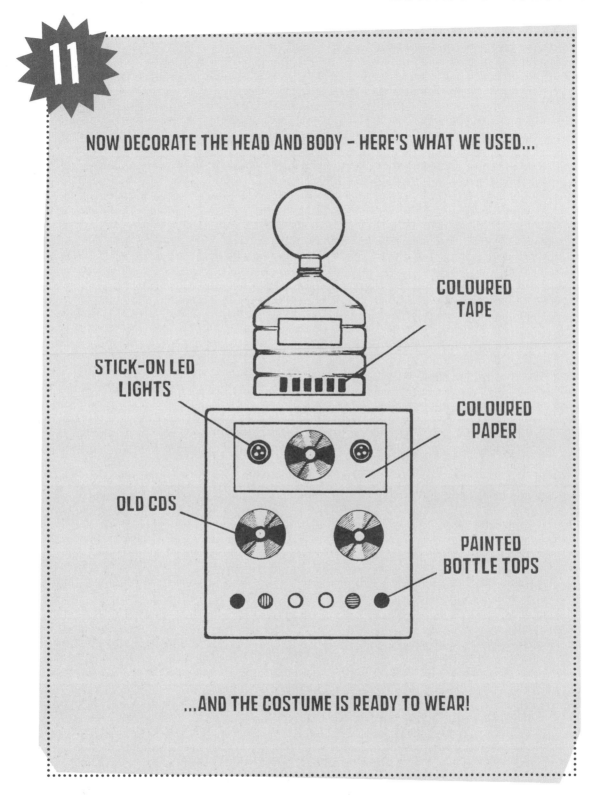

COLOURED TAPE

STICK-ON LED LIGHTS

COLOURED PAPER

OLD CDS

PAINTED BOTTLE TOPS

...AND THE COSTUME IS READY TO WEAR!

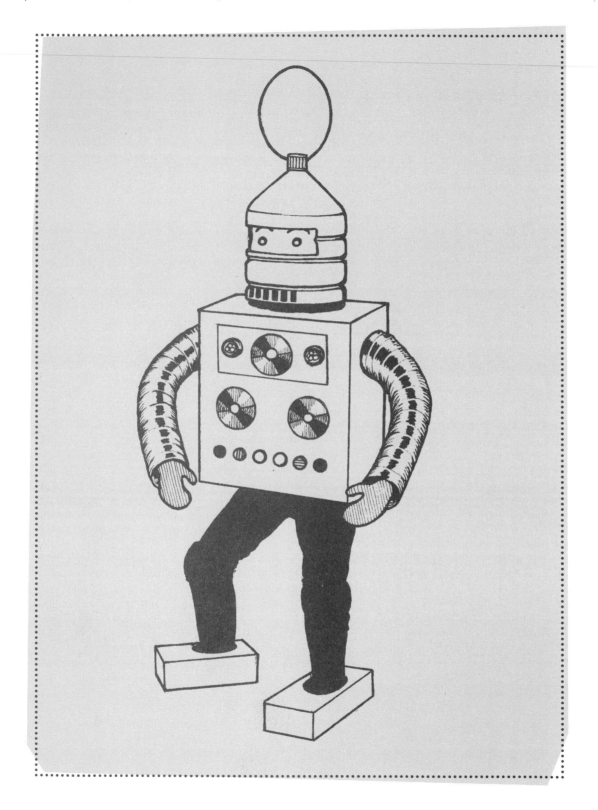

GET DAD TO HELP PUT THE COSTUME ON. CHARLIE WORE GREY GLOVES, OLD BLACK JOGGING BOTTOMS AND OLD SKATE KNEEPADS. WHERE YOUR FACE SHOWS THROUGH THE EYE-SLOT, TRY PUTTING ON SILVER FACE PAINT. PRACTISE YOUR ROBOT WALK AND VOICE AND – WHO KNOWS – YOU MIGHT EVEN CONVINCE OTHER ROBOTS!

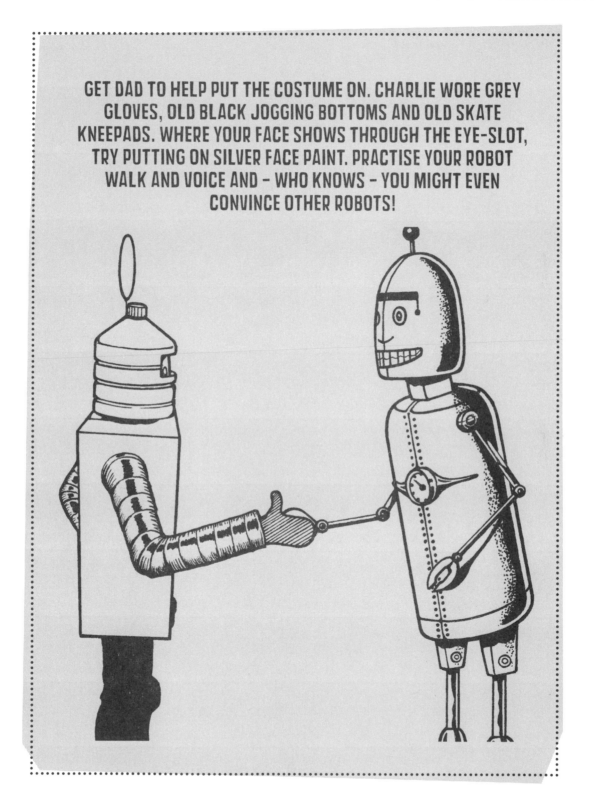

PROJECT 3:
JETPACK

THE MUST-HAVE GADGET FOR THE BUSY, MODERN
ROBOT IN A RUSH! THIS IS EASY TO MAKE
AND ALL YOU NEED IS:
STURDY CARDBOARD BOX
(ABOUT THE SIZE OF A BACKPACK)
TWO STRIPS OF CARDBOARD
FROM A FLATTENED BOX
TWO EMPTY TWO LITRE COLA BOTTLES
TWO EMPTY 500 ML WATER BOTTLES
TWO EQUAL LENGTHS OF OLD ELECTRICAL FLEX
STUFF TO DECORATE

1

TAPE THE STRIPS OF CARDBOARD TO THE BOX IN LOOPS. ADJUST THE LENGTH TO FIT YOU...

2

THEN TAPE TWO EQUAL LENGTHS OF ELECTRIC CABLE TO THE SIDES. IN EACH WATER BOTTLE, PUNCH A HOLE, FEED THE CABLE THROUGH AND TIE A KNOT. PUSH THE KNOT BACK INTO THE BOTTLE AND REPLACE THE LID. THESE ARE YOUR HAND CONTROLS.

3

TAPE THE COLA BOTTLES TO THE BACK OF THE BOX – UPSIDE DOWN.

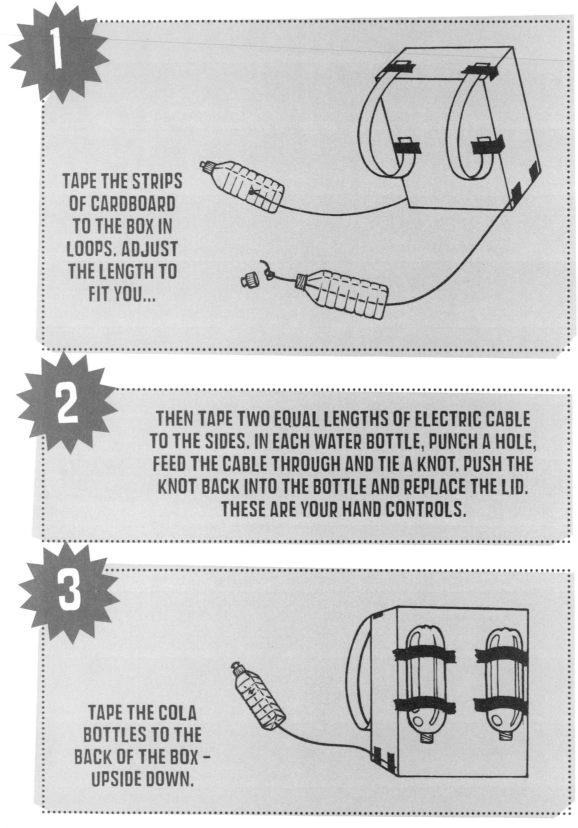

4

DECORATE – WE PAINTED OURS BLACK WITH YELLOW BOTTLES AND ADDED DIALS. WE ALSO GLUED ON SOME CIRCUIT BOARDS FROM AN OLD BROKEN STEREO. MAKE SURE EVERYONE IS STANDING WELL BACK WHEN YOU TAKE OFF! WHOOSH!!!

PROJECT 4:
LUNAR ROVER

DO YOU HAVE ANY OLD TOYS THAT YOU NO LONGER
PLAY WITH? HAVE A LOOK IN YOUR TOY BOX TO
SEE IF THERE'S ANYTHING YOU COULD RECYCLE
TO MAKE A NEW TOY.

I DUG OUT MY OLD RADIO-CONTROLLED BUGGY AND
DAD HELPED ME TO REINVENT IT AS A LUNAR ROVER.
WE USED A PIECE OF STIFF CARD AND THE CLEAR DOME
LID FROM A MILKSHAKE CUP AND I MADE A ROBOT
EXPLORER'S HEAD FROM MODELLING CLAY
TO DRIVE THE ROVER.

FIRSTLY, DAD REMOVED THE BODY FROM THE BUGGY
WITH A SCREWDRIVER. THEN WE CUT A SQUARE OF CARD
AND FIXED IT TO THE CHASSIS WITH ELECTRICAL TAPE.

WE STUCK THE HEAD TO THE CARD AND GLUED THE DOME
OVER THE TOP. SIMPLE! OF COURSE, YOU MAY NOT HAVE
A BUGGY LIKE THIS, BUT SEE WHAT YOU CAN ADAPT,
RECYCLE AND GIVE A NEW LEASE OF LIFE TO...

36

PROJECT 5 :
PROPELLERHEAD

SOMEONE IS IN A SPIN! PROPELLERHEAD IS MADE FROM A LARGE DETERGENT BOTTLE – THE TYPE WITH A CUT-AWAY HANDLE. THE PROPELLERS ARE A LITTLE HAND HELD, BATTERY OPERATED FAN FROM A GIFT STORE. WE MADE ARMS FROM CARDBOARD AND MILK BOTTLE TOPS. WE ALSO USED STICKY TAPE, A CRAFT KNIFE, GLUE, AND DAD SPRAY-PAINTED THE BOTTLE.

1

HAVING SPRAY-PAINTED THE BOTTLE WE FITTED THE FAN INTO THE 'NECK'. OUR FAN DIDN'T FIT SNUGLY, SO WE WRAPPED ELECTRICAL TAPE ROUND ITS MIDDLE UNTIL IT DID...

2

THE BUTTON TO TURN THE FAN ON WAS NOW INSIDE THE BOTTLE SO WE CUT AWAY A SECTION FROM THE BOTTOM.

3

FOR ARMS WE CUT TWO 'BOOMERANG' SHAPES FROM STIFF CARD. TO THESE WE STUCK MILK BOTTLE CAPS, THEN GLUED THE ARMS TO THE SIDES OF THE BOTTLE AND LASTLY DECORATED IT.

4

'YOU LOOK STRANGELY FAMILIAR'

'I'M YOUR BIGGEST FAN'

PROJECT 6: ROCKET LAUNCHER

PROFESSOR ZIPPY WILL NOW SHOW YOU HOW TO LAUNCH A ROBOT INTO ORBIT IN HIS OWN ROCKET! YOU'LL DEFINITELY NEED DAD'S HELP WITH THIS PROJECT AS IT INVOLVES A REAL PROPELLED MISSILE. THE LAUNCH SHOULD BE CONDUCTED OUT OF DOORS AND ON A DAY WITH LITTLE OR NO WIND.

YOU WILL NEED: A 35MM PHOTOGRAPHIC FILM CANISTER (IT SHOULD BE THE TYPE WHOSE LID SNAPS SHUT INSIDE THE CANISTER AND IS AIRTIGHT. YOU SHOULD BE ABLE TO GET ONE FROM YOUR LOCAL FILM DEVELOPING SHOP), THE CARDBOARD TUBE FROM A KITCHEN ROLL, A SHEET OF A4 CARD, AN ALKA SELTZER TABLET, A TEA TRAY OR OTHER FLAT SURFACE (FOR YOUR LAUNCH PAD), WATER, STICKY TAPE AND SCISSORS.

1

TAPE THE CANISTER INSIDE THE TUBE WITH THE OPEN END FACING OUT.

2

CUT A CIRCLE FROM THE CARD, AND CUT A SECTION AWAY. ROLL THIS INTO A CONE SHAPE AND TAPE IT TOGETHER. THEN TAPE IT ONTO THE TUBE (AT THE OPPOSITE END TO THE CANISTER).

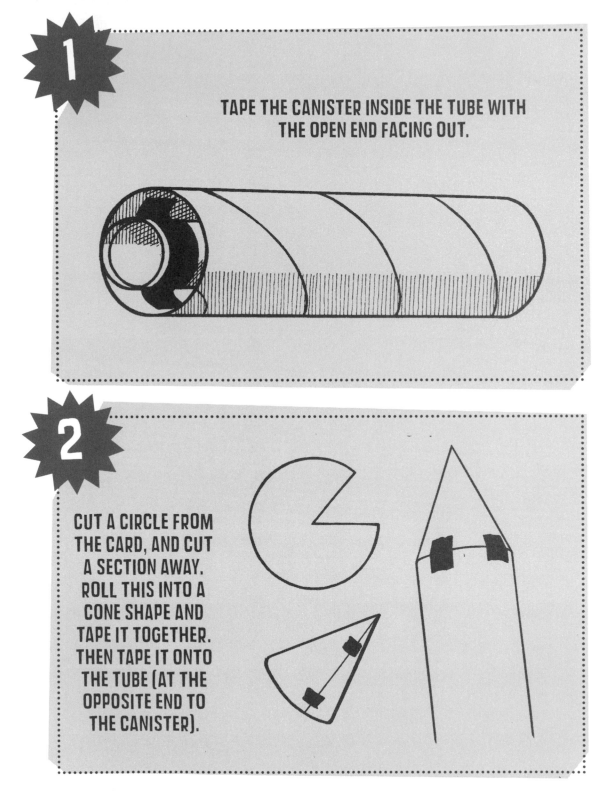

3

CUT OUT THREE MATCHING TRIANGLES OF CARD. FOLD THEM ALONG ONE EDGE AND TAPE THEM TO THE 'ENGINE' END OF THE ROCKET.

x 3

4

DRAW A ROBOT FACE INSIDE A CIRCLE (LIKE A PORTHOLE). CUT IT OUT AND STICK IT ON TO THE SIDE OF THE ROCKET.

NOW IT'S OVER TO DAD FOR THE LAUNCH! DAD – YOU SHOULD WEAR PROTECTIVE EYEWEAR AND BE SURE EVERYONE ELSE STANDS WELL BACK. BLU-TAC A PIECE OF ALKA-SELTZER (ABOUT A QUARTER OF A TABLET) TO THE INSIDE OF THE LID OF THE CANISTER.

HOLD THE ROCKET UPSIDE DOWN AND CAREFULLY POUR A LITTLE WATER INTO THE CANISTER – IT SHOULD BE JUST UNDER HALF FULL. SNAP THE LID ON THE CANISTER, TURN THE ROCKET THE RIGHT WAY UP, SET IT ON THE LAUNCH PAD AND STAND WELL BACK. WE HAVE LIFT OFF! SO HOW DOES IT WORK, PROFESSOR ZIPPY?

'WHEN THE ALKA SELTZER DISSOLVES IT GIVES OFF BUBBLES OF CARBON DIOXIDE GAS. THE GAS BUILDS UP UNTIL THE PRESSURE IS SO GREAT THAT IT FORCES THE LID OFF AND PROPELS THE ROCKET.'

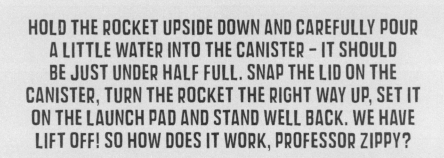

PROJECT 7: *LITTLE CLAY ROBOTS*

ART STORES SELL SOME BRILLIANT TYPES OF MODELLING CLAY IN LOTS OF COLOURS. SOME ARE AIR-DRYING AND OTHERS ARE HARDENED IN THE OVEN. THERE ARE NO LIMITS TO THE SHAPES YOU CAN MAKE AND THE CLAY CAN BE COMBINED WITH OTHER MATERIALS. FOR EXAMPLE, THE LITTLE ROBOT OPPOSITE HAS A COUPLE OF OLD SCREWS FOR LEGS, WASHERS FOR HANDS AND AN OLD ELECTRIC MOTOR FROM A SLOT CAR FOR A HEAD.

SHOPS WHERE YOU CAN BUY THE CLAY USUALLY SELL ACCESSORIES THAT ALLOW YOU TO MAKE YOUR CLAY MODEL INTO A BADGE, BROOCH, OR KEY-RING.

52

PROJECT 8: *ARTICULATED WALL ROBOT*

THIS ROBOT IS CONSTRUCTED FROM FLAT CARD SHAPES, JOINED WITH PAPER FASTENERS. WHEN HUNG ON THE WALL, THE HEAD, ARMS AND LEGS CAN BE MOVED TO DIFFERENT POSITIONS. YOU COULD MAKE IT ANY SIZE BUT WE RECOMMEND A PIECE OF CARD ABOUT 40 X 30 CMS. FROM THIS STARTING POINT, CUT SHAPES FOR THE HEAD, ARMS, LEGS, HANDS AND FEET. WE'VE DRAWN A TEMPLATE YOU MAY FOLLOW.

YOU WILL NEED: CARD, SCISSORS OR A CRAFT KNIFE, RULER, HOLE PUNCH, PAPER FASTENERS, PAINT OR COLOURED PAPER TO DECORATE, PINS OR POSTER-TACK TO FIX TO THE WALL.

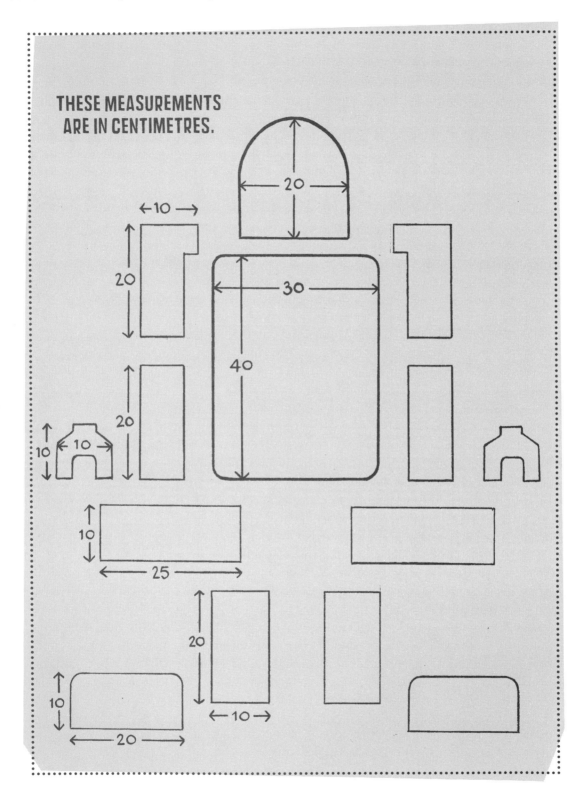

THESE MEASUREMENTS
ARE IN CENTIMETRES.

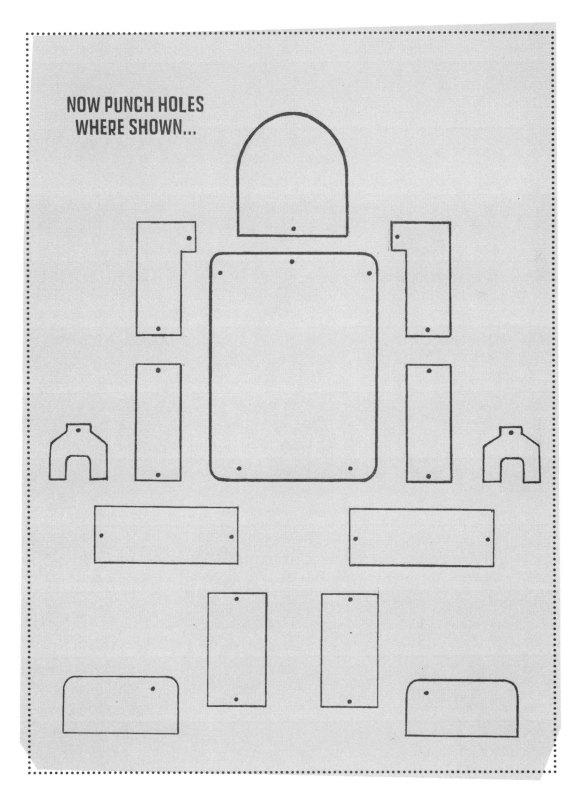

NOW PUNCH HOLES
WHERE SHOWN...

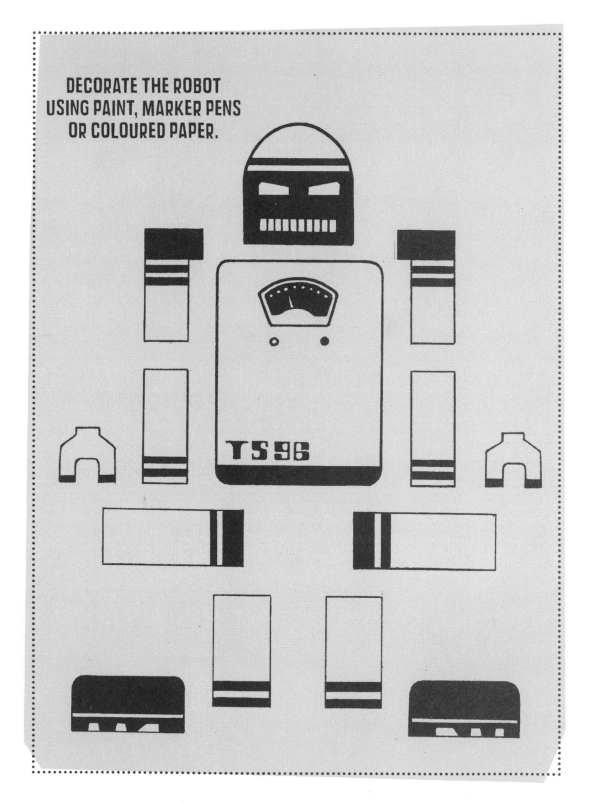

DECORATE THE ROBOT USING PAINT, MARKER PENS OR COLOURED PAPER.

JOIN THE PIECES TOGETHER WITH PAPER FASTENERS.
AS HE'S ARTICULATED HE CAN BE PINNED TO THE WALL IN
VARIOUS POSITIONS – YOU CAN MAKE HIM LOOK LIKE HE'S
WALKING, SITTING, CHASING OR EVEN DANCING!

PROJECT 9:
THE TIN MAN

ALTHOUGH THE TIN MAN CHARACTER WAS ACTUALLY CREATED BEFORE THE TERM ROBOT WAS EVEN COINED, WE THINK HE'S ONE OF THE FIRST MODERN ROBOTS. OUR TIN MAN IS A BIT FISHY! FOUR OF THE CANS WE USED WERE PILCHARD CANS AND TWO CONTAINED TUNA. WE WASHED THEM VERY THOROUGHLY BEFORE WE STARTED!

HERE'S EVERYTHING WE USED: LARGE CATERING SIZE TIN CAN FOR THE BODY, FOUR REGULAR BEAN CANS FOR LEGS, FOUR SMALL PILCHARD CANS FOR ARMS, TWO TUNA CANS FOR THE HEAD, PLASTIC FUNNEL (ABOUT THE SAME WIDTH AS THE TUNA CANS), TWO OLD FORKS, TWO WIRE COAT HANGERS, TWO CORKS, STICKY FOAM SPACER-TAPE. AND FROM THE TOOLBOX: DRILL, WIRE SNIPPERS, PLIERS, HACKSAW, STRONG TAPE.

1

STAND THE LARGEST TIN UPSIDE DOWN. NEAR THE BOTTOM* DRILL TWO HOLES ABOUT 4CMS APART. THEN DO THE SAME ON THE OPPOSITE SIDE.

*(OPEN END)

2

TAKE TWO OF THE BEAN CANS AND DRILL HOLES IN THE SAME WAY – NEAR THE OPEN END AND AGAIN, 4CMS APART.

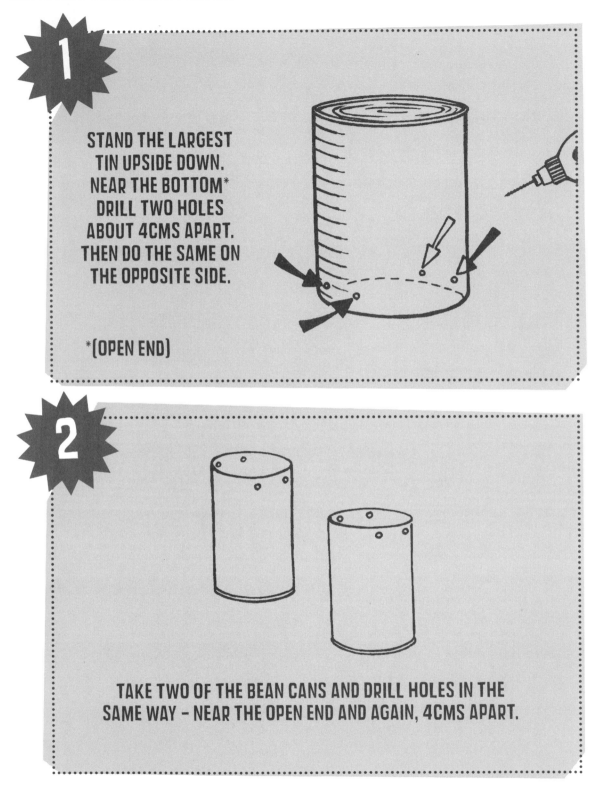

3

CUT TWO LENGTHS OF COAT HANGER WIRE A LITTLE WIDER THAN THE 'BODY' TIN. FEED THESE THROUGH THE HOLES OF ALL THREE CANS.

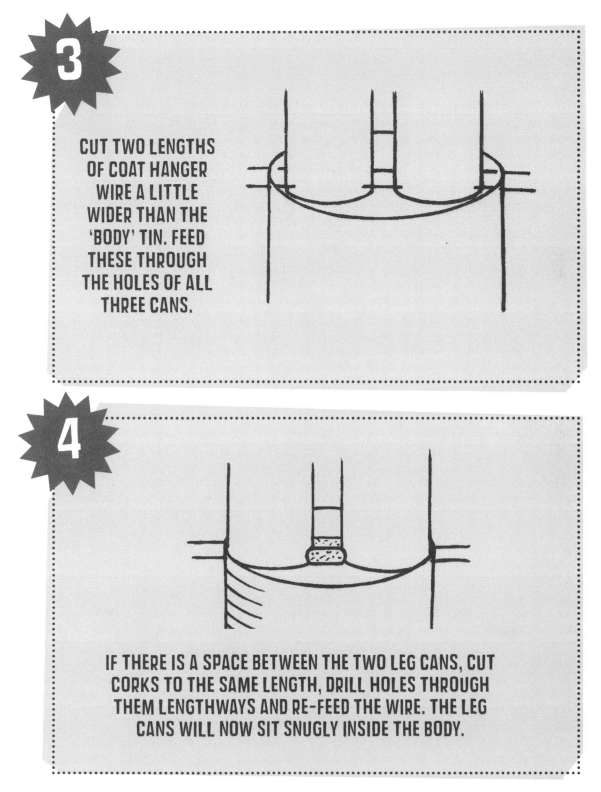

4

IF THERE IS A SPACE BETWEEN THE TWO LEG CANS, CUT CORKS TO THE SAME LENGTH, DRILL HOLES THROUGH THEM LENGTHWAYS AND RE-FEED THE WIRE. THE LEG CANS WILL NOW SIT SNUGLY INSIDE THE BODY.

5

USING PLIERS, BEND THE ENDS OF THE WIRE AND TUCK THEM SAFELY UNDER THE BODY.

6

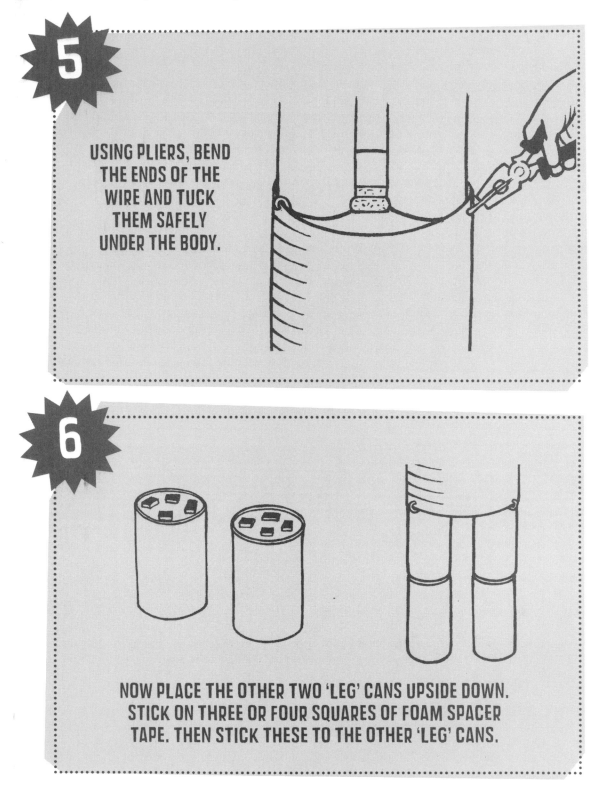

NOW PLACE THE OTHER TWO 'LEG' CANS UPSIDE DOWN. STICK ON THREE OR FOUR SQUARES OF FOAM SPACER TAPE. THEN STICK THESE TO THE OTHER 'LEG' CANS.

7

NOW DRILL TWO HOLES NEAR THE TOP OF THE BODY AND FEED THROUGH A LENGTH OF WIRE (ABOUT 65CM). BEND A 90° ANGLE ABOUT 3CM FROM THE BODY ON EITHER SIDE.

8

DRILL A HOLE, CENTRALLY, IN THE BOTTOMS OF THE FOUR SMALLER CANS AND DRILL LENGTHWAYS THROUGH FOUR CORKS. FEED A CAN ONTO THE WIRE, THEN A CORK (PUSH THE CORK RIGHT INSIDE THE CAN). DO THE SAME WITH A SECOND CAN AND CORK – THEN REPEAT FOR THE OPPOSITE ARM.

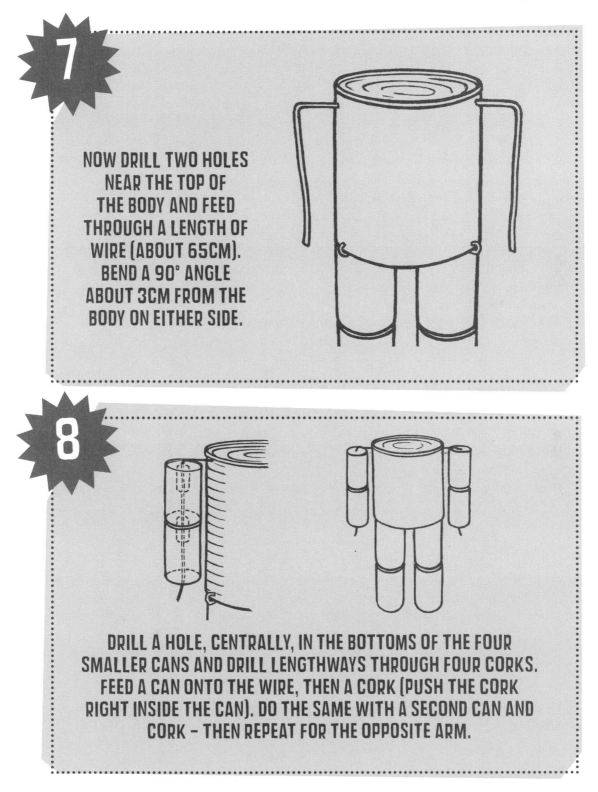

9

CAREFULLY CUT OFF THE HANDLES OF THE OLD FORKS WITH A HACKSAW! DISCARD THE HANDLES AND TAPE THE FORKS TO THE ENDS OF THE WIRE.

10

GLUE TOGETHER THE TWO TUNA CANS AND THE FUNNEL TO MAKE THE HEAD AND GLUE IT TO THE BODY.

FINALLY, DECORATE HIM USING STICKERS. WE GAVE OUR TIN MAN A HEART. WHICH IS WHY HE LOOKS SO HAPPY.

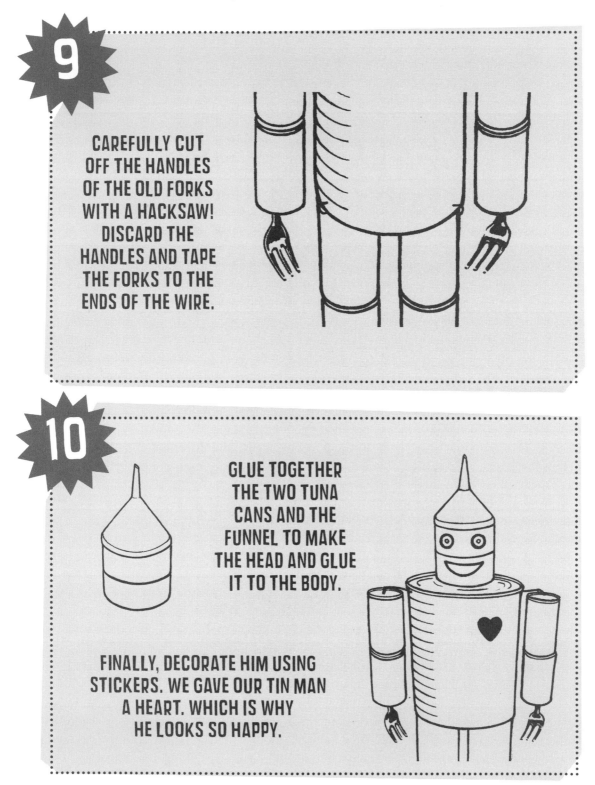

PROJECT 10:
HERBIE
(THE GROWING ROBOT)

HERBIE IS SO-CALLED BECAUSE HIS HAIR IS A LIVING THYME PLANT. HE IS MADE FROM TWO PLASTIC PLANT POTS, ONE ABOUT TWICE THE SIZE OF THE OTHER. THE HEAD POT SHOULD BE ROUGHLY THE SAME SIZE AS THAT OF THE PLANT YOU'VE CHOSEN. HIS ARMS ARE MADE FROM TWO BENDY DRINKING STRAWS, HIS HANDS FROM SELF-DRYING MODELLING CLAY AND OLD WIRE.

FROM DAD'S TOOL BOX, YOU'LL NEED:
A DRILL AND SOME WIRE SNIPPERS.

1

STAND THE LARGER POT UPSIDE DOWN. GET DAD TO DRILL TWO HOLES, ONE IN EACH SIDE, JUST BIG ENOUGH FOR A STRAW TO FIT IN.

2

PAINT EACH POT GREY WITH A MATT HOUSEHOLD PAINT. IF YOU WANT A SMOOTHER FINISH DAD COULD SPRAY-PAINT THEM.

3

WHEN THIS PAINT IS DRY, PAINT THE RIM OF EACH POT WITH A GLOSS PAINT SUCH AS MODELLER'S ENAMEL (RED WOULD LOOK GOOD) AND ALLOW TO DRY.

4

NEXT, PAINT OR STICK ON YOUR DETAILS. REMEMBER THE BIG 'BODY' POT WILL BE UPSIDE DOWN, THE 'HEAD' POT THE RIGHT WAY UP.

5

JOIN TOGETHER TWO BENDY STRAWS AT LONG ENDS. FEED THEM THROUGH THE HOLES YOU MADE IN THE BODY TO MAKE ARMS.

6

ROLL TWO EQUALLY SIZED BALLS OF MODELLING CLAY FOR THE HANDS AND PUSH THEM ONTO THE ARMS. ADD FINGERS BY CUTTING SHORT LENGTHS OF THICK FUSE WIRE, BEND SLIGHTLY AND PUSH INTO THE HANDS.

7

EASE YOUR CHOSEN PLANT FROM ITS POT AND RE-PLANT IN THE HEAD. WHEN YOU'VE DECIDED WHERE IT'S GOING TO LIVE, PLACE THE BODY ON A TRAY AND SIT THE HEAD ON TOP – WHEN YOU WATER THE PLANT THE WATER WILL DRAIN THROUGH THE BODY INTO THE TRAY. YOU COULD MAKE A HERB GARDEN WITH A ROBOT FOR EACH HERB. OTHER HOUSE PLANTS ARE GOOD TOO. A SPIDER PLANT MAKES A NICE SPIKEY HAIRCUT! IT'S AN EASY PLANT TO KEEP AND IS GOOD AT CLEANING THE AIR.

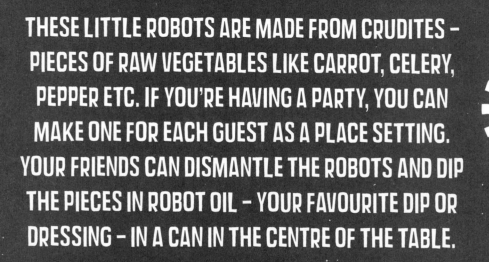

PROJECT 11:

EDIBLE PARTY ROBOTS

THESE LITTLE ROBOTS ARE MADE FROM CRUDITES – PIECES OF RAW VEGETABLES LIKE CARROT, CELERY, PEPPER ETC. IF YOU'RE HAVING A PARTY, YOU CAN MAKE ONE FOR EACH GUEST AS A PLACE SETTING. YOUR FRIENDS CAN DISMANTLE THE ROBOTS AND DIP THE PIECES IN ROBOT OIL – YOUR FAVOURITE DIP OR DRESSING – IN A CAN IN THE CENTRE OF THE TABLE.

ALL YOU NEED IS YOUR CHOICE OF VEGETABLES, CUT INTO SHAPES AND SOME COCKTAIL STICKS TO JOIN THE PARTS TOGETHER. HERE ARE A COUPLE OF EXAMPLES TO SHOW YOU WHAT WE USED.

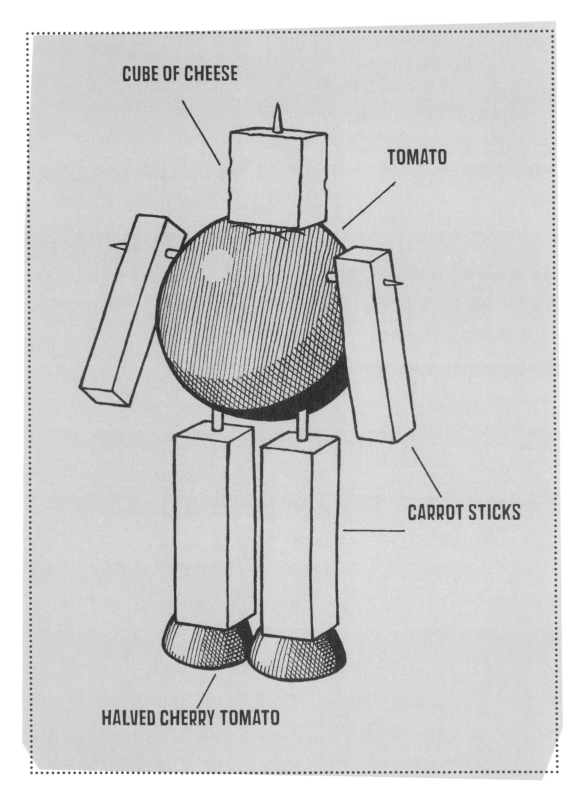

CUBE OF CHEESE

TOMATO

CARROT STICKS

HALVED CHERRY TOMATO

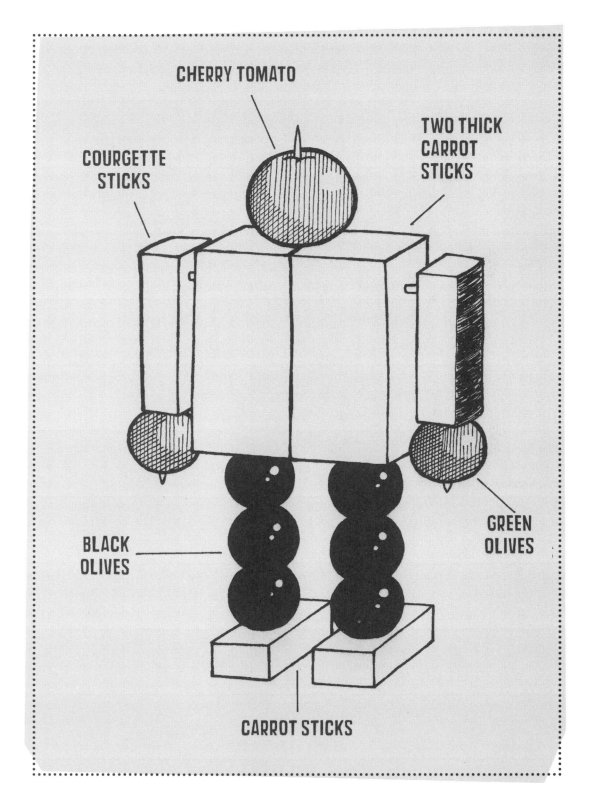

CHERRY TOMATO

TWO THICK CARROT STICKS

COURGETTE STICKS

GREEN OLIVES

BLACK OLIVES

CARROT STICKS

REPLACE THE LABELS ON SOME USED, WASHED TIN CANS
WITH YOUR OWN LABEL WITH THE WORDS 'ROBOT OIL'
AND FILL THESE WITH THE DIPS OF YOUR CHOICE.

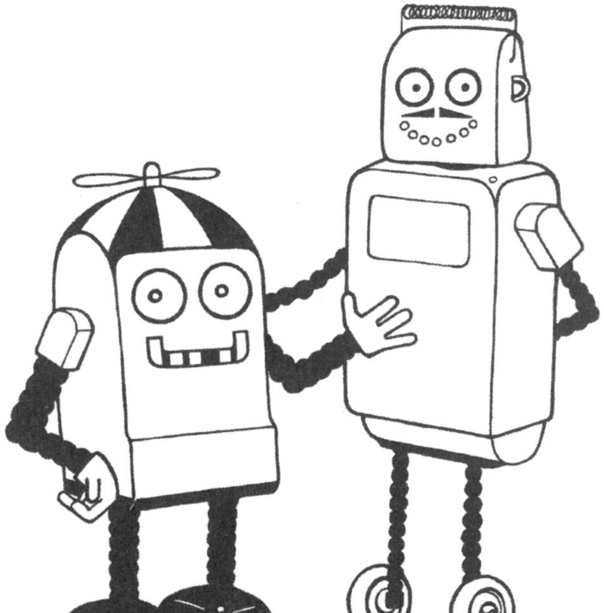

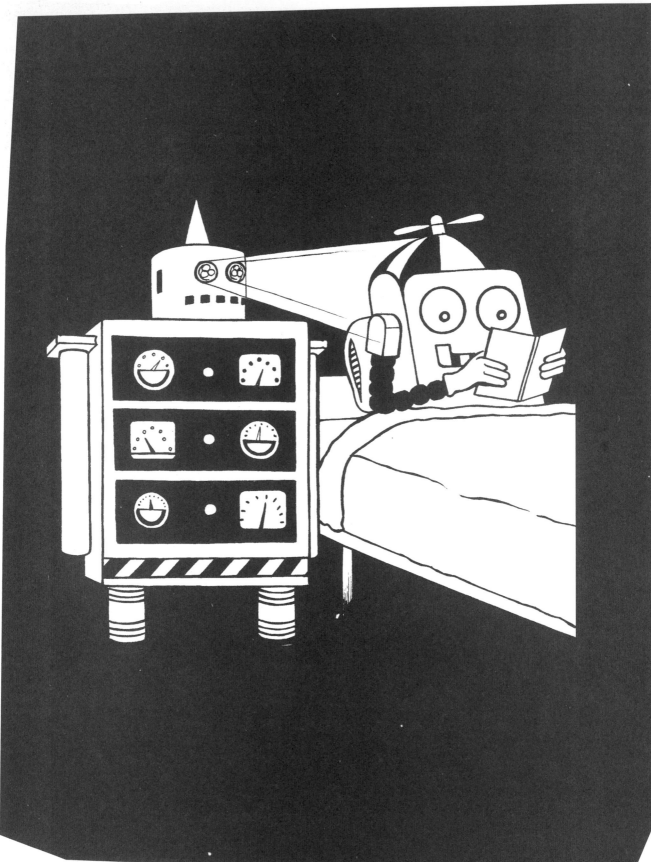

PROJECT 12:
BEDSIDE ROBOT

HERE IS A PROJECT WHICH GIVES NEW LIFE TO AN OLD BEDSIDE CABINET. WE USED OLD CARDBOARD TUBES (FABRIC SHOPS THROW THESE AWAY) FOR ARMS. THE HEAD WAS MADE FROM A ROUND BISCUIT TIN WITH STICKY-BACKED LED LIGHTS FOR EYES (FROM THE GIFT STORE).

DAD WILL NEED HIS DRILL AND A SAW.
ALSO: SANDER OR SANDPAPER
FOUR NUTS AND BOLTS
HOUSEHOLD PAINT
STRONG GLUE

1

FIRSTLY, DAD PREPARED OUR CABINET FOR PAINTING BY SANDING IT LIGHTLY ALL OVER – HE DID IT OUTSIDE.

2

CUT TWO LENGTHS OF CARDBOARD TUBE FOR ARMS USING A SAW. THE CUTS SHOULD BE NICE AND EVEN SO YOU CAN GLUE BOOKS ON FOR 'SHOULDERS'. THE LENGTH OF THE ARMS SHOULD BE LESS THAN THE HEIGHT OF THE CABINET.

3

DRILL A HOLE BIG ENOUGH FOR YOUR BOLTS
ABOUT AN INCH FROM EACH END OF THE ARMS.
MAKE SURE THE HOLES ARE IN A LINE.

4

REMOVE THE DRAWERS AND DRILL CORRESPONDING
HOLES IN THE SIDES OF THE CABINET. ATTACH THE
ARMS WITH THE NUTS AND BOLTS.

5

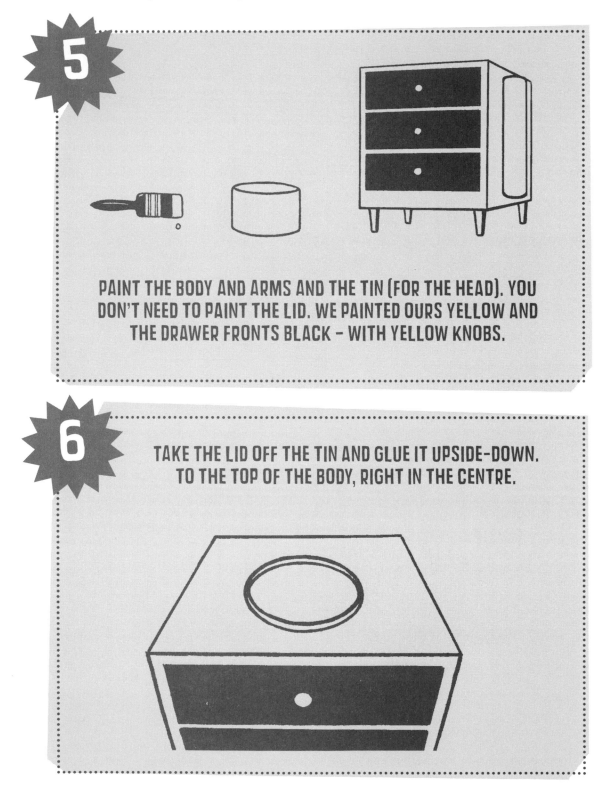

PAINT THE BODY AND ARMS AND THE TIN (FOR THE HEAD). YOU
DON'T NEED TO PAINT THE LID. WE PAINTED OURS YELLOW AND
THE DRAWER FRONTS BLACK – WITH YELLOW KNOBS.

6

TAKE THE LID OFF THE TIN AND GLUE IT UPSIDE-DOWN.
TO THE TOP OF THE BODY, RIGHT IN THE CENTRE.

7

PLACE THE TIN UPSIDE-DOWN IN THE LID AND ATTACH THE LED 'EYES'. THE HEAD REVOLVES SO YOU CAN POINT THE LIGHT WHERE YOU CHOOSE.

8

IF YOUR CABINET HAS LEGS YOU CAN GIVE THE ROBOT LEGS MADE FROM TIN CAN. CHOOSE TWO CANS ABOUT THE SAME HEIGHT AS THE LEGS, DECORATE AS DESIRED AND SIMPLY STAND THE FRONT LEGS IN THEM.

9

FIX THE HARDBACK BOOKS TO THE TOP OF THE ARMS WITH STRONG GLUE. THESE WILL MAKE A USEFUL LITTLE SHELF YOU CAN PUT YOUR BEDTIME BOOK ON. FINALLY, DECORATE THE ROBOT. WE STUCK A CARDBOARD CONE TO THE HEAD (FROM THE MIDDLE OF A ROLL OF YARN) AND PAINTED ON DIALS ETC. BLACK AND YELLOW HAZARD TAPE LOOKS GOOD TOO.

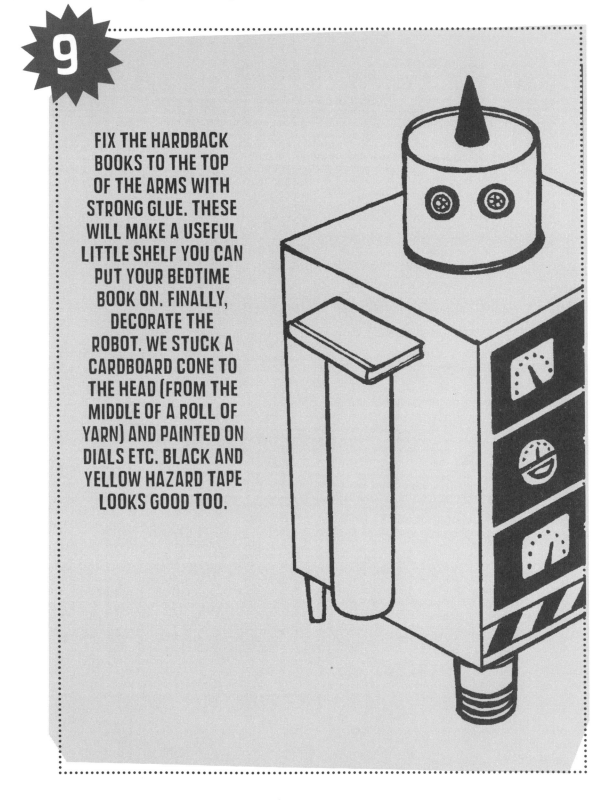

PROJECT 13:
THE CHAMP

THIS LITTLE ROBOT IS A BIT OF A PUSHOVER – BUT HE'LL ALWAYS GET UP AGAIN! TO MAKE HIM YOU'LL NEED THREE PIECES OF A4 CARD, A SQUARISH CARDBOARD CARTON (AROUND 10 CM WIDE AT MOST) AND A SHORT LENGTH OF BENDY CURTAIN WIRE WITH SCREW-IN EYE LOOPS.

YOU'LL ALSO NEED:
REGULAR ROUND PARTY BALLOON
WHOLE PACK OF DRIED PULSES
TWO MATCHING BOTTLE TOPS FOR EYES
TWO MATCHING BOTTLE TOPS FOR EARS
PAPER MACHE (SEE PAGE 13)
STICKY TAPE, SCISSORS,
PAPER GLUE.

1

TAPE TWO SHEETS OF CARD TOGETHER THEN
TAPE EACH END TOGETHER TO FORM A CYLINDER.

2

BLOW UP A BALLOON TO ABOUT THE SAME
CIRCUMFERENCE AS THE CYLINDER – SO THE
BALLOON SITS SNUGLY ON THE TOP.

3

NOW COVER THE WHOLE THING WITH PAPER MACHE
(SEE PAGE 13). WHEN THE PAPER MACHE IS COMPLETELY
DRY, TAKE A PIN AND POP THE BALLOON.

4

YOU NOW HAVE A CYLINDER
WITH A DOME SHAPE AT ONE END.
WEIGHT THE DOMED END BY
POURING IN A WHOLE PACK OF
DRIED PULSES, SUCH AS KIDNEY
BEANS AND SEAL THEM IN WITH
A FLAT LAYER OF PAPER MACHE.
ALLOW TO DRY.

DRIED BEANS

LAYER OF PAPER
MACHE

5

MAKE TWO HOLES JUST BIG ENOUGHTO FEED THROUGH THE CURTAIN WIRE TO MAKE TWO EQUAL LENGTH ARMS – THEN SCREW THE 'EYES' INTO THE ENDS OF THE WIRE TO MAKE HANDS.

6

ON THE REMAINING SHEET OF CARD, DRAW A CIRCLE THE SAME DIAMETER AS THE BODY (YOU CAN DRAW ROUND THE BODY). DRAW SOME TABS OUTSIDE THE CIRCLE THEN CUT IT OUT. STICK THE SQUARE CARTON TO THE CENTRE OF THE CIRCLE.

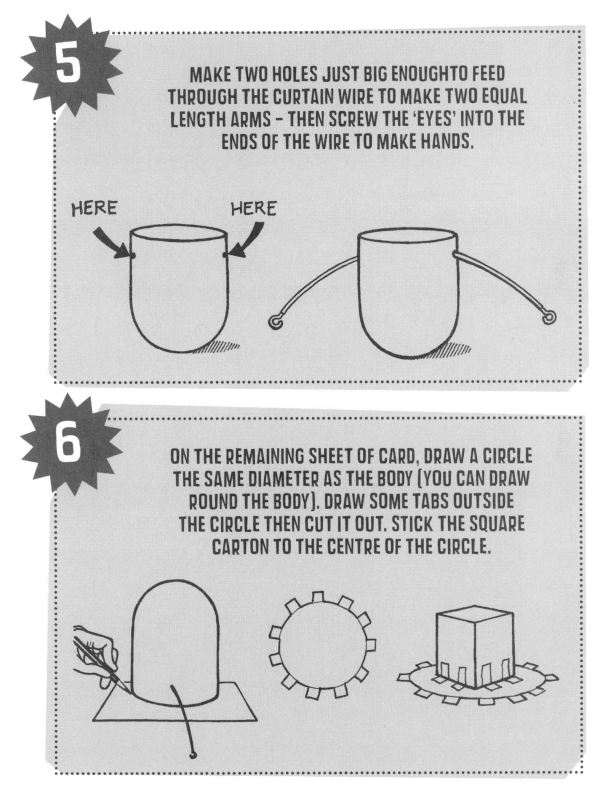

7

FOLD THE TABS OVER AND STICK TO THE BODY BY GLUING THE TABS OR TAPING OVER THEM.

8

STICK BOTTLE TOPS TO THE HEAD TO MAKE EYES AND EARS. THEN USE PAPER MACHE TO COVER THE HEAD AND STRENGTHEN THE JOINS AT THE TOP OF THE BODY.

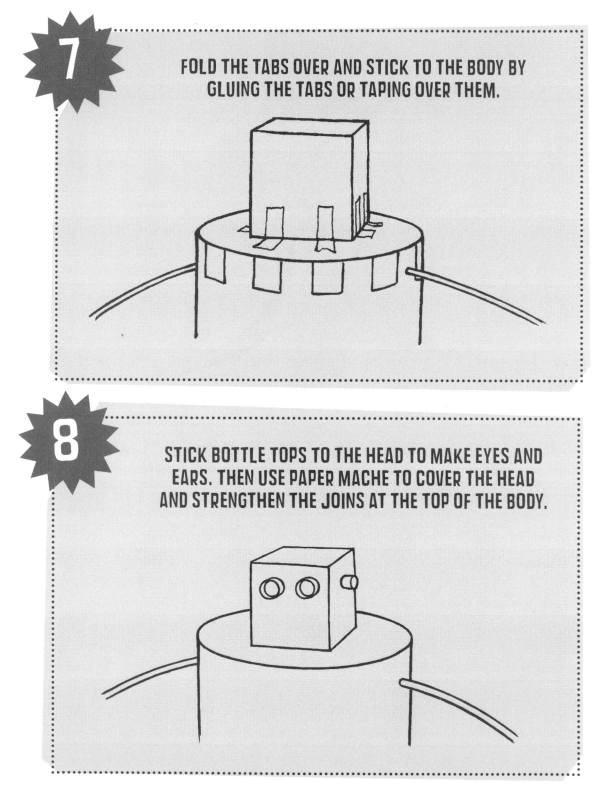

9

FINALLY, PAINT AND DECORATE AS YOU CHOOSE. HOWEVER MUCH YOU PUSH HIM. YOU'LL FIND HE ALWAYS ENDS UP STANDING!

NOTHING GETS ME DOWN!

PROJECT 14:
ART BOX

OUR ART BOX HAS LOTS OF SPACE TO STORE YOUR STATIONERY. WE SAVED UP MATCHBOXES – EIGHT LARGE 'COOKS' MATCHBOXES AND 10 REGULAR ONES. THESE MAKE THE BODY AND LEGS. THE HEAD IS AN ORDINARY BEAN CAN AND THE ARMS ARE MADE FROM CARDBOARD TUBE FROM THE MIDDLE OF A ROLL OF KITCHEN PAPER.

WE ALSO USED:
STICKY TAPE
PAPER MACHE (SEE PAGE 13)
PAPER FASTENERS

1 TAPE SIX OF THE MATCHBOXES TOGETHER IN A BLOCK LIKE THIS TO MAKE THE BODY.

2 THEN TAPE TOGETHER TWO BLOCKS FOR LEGS, EACH MADE FROM FIVE REGULAR MATCHBOXES.

3 STICK THE LEGS TO THE REMAINING TWO LARGE MATCHBOXES, THEN STICK THE LEGS TO THE BODY.

4

CAREFULLY CUT THE CARDBOARD TUBE IN HALF WITH A CRAFT KNIFE AND TAPE PAPER OVER ONE END OF EACH HALF.

5

THEN TAPE EACH OF THESE (OPEN UPWARDS) TO THE SIDES OF THE BODY.

6

LASTLY, TAPE THE CAN ON TOP OF THE BODY (RIGHT WAY UP) FOR A HEAD.

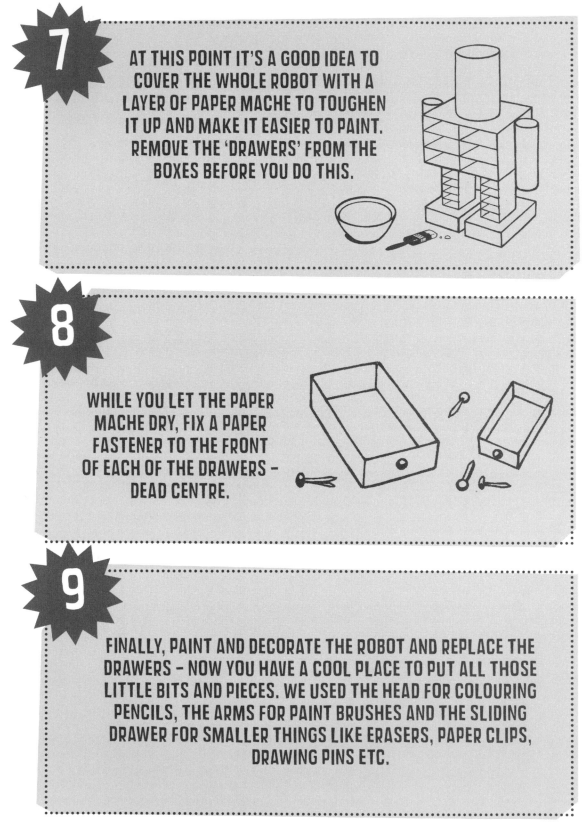

7 AT THIS POINT IT'S A GOOD IDEA TO COVER THE WHOLE ROBOT WITH A LAYER OF PAPER MACHE TO TOUGHEN IT UP AND MAKE IT EASIER TO PAINT. REMOVE THE 'DRAWERS' FROM THE BOXES BEFORE YOU DO THIS.

8 WHILE YOU LET THE PAPER MACHE DRY, FIX A PAPER FASTENER TO THE FRONT OF EACH OF THE DRAWERS – DEAD CENTRE.

9 FINALLY, PAINT AND DECORATE THE ROBOT AND REPLACE THE DRAWERS – NOW YOU HAVE A COOL PLACE TO PUT ALL THOSE LITTLE BITS AND PIECES. WE USED THE HEAD FOR COLOURING PENCILS, THE ARMS FOR PAINT BRUSHES AND THE SLIDING DRAWER FOR SMALLER THINGS LIKE ERASERS, PAPER CLIPS, DRAWING PINS ETC.

PROJECT 15:
SPRINGTIME WITH MR WIBBLE

MISTER WIBBLE LIKES TO WOBBLE! HIS ARMS AND LEGS ARE MADE FROM SPRINGS. WE USED OLD MATTRESS SPRINGS FOR THE LEGS AND MADE OUR OWN SPRINGS FOR THE ARMS. HIS BODY IS AN OLD COFFEE CAN AND HIS HEAD IS THE PLASTIC DOMED LID OF A TAKEAWAY COFFEE / MILKSHAKE CUP. YOU'LL NEED THE WIRE FROM A DISCARDED ELECTRICAL APPLIANCE LIKE A BROKEN TOASTER OR LAMP TO MAKE THE ARM SPRINGS AND A BLOCK OF WOOD FOR A BASE.

YOU'LL ALSO NEED: PLIERS, WIRE SNIPPERS, AWL, SMALL HAMMER , SOME U-NAILS, CRAFT KNIFE, GLUE.

1

REMOVE THE LABEL FROM THE COFFEE CAN. OUR CAN WAS THE 'PAINTED' TYPE SO WE COVERED IT WITH SHINY SILVER MARINE TAPE.

2

TO MAKE THE ARMS, CUT THE CABLE FROM YOUR BROKEN APPLIANCE (CUT THE PLUG OFF FIRST!). USE A CRAFT KNIFE TO STRIP AWAY THE OUTER PLASTIC COATING AND DISCARD.

3

TWIST TOGETHER FOUR LENGTHS OF THE INNER WIRES TO MAKE ONE STIFFER WIRE. COIL THIS AROUND A JUMBO MARKER PEN TO MAKE A SPRING. REPEAT FOR THE SECOND ARM.

4

PUNCH A HOLE EITHER SIDE OF THE CAN WITH AN AWL. FEED ONE END OF THE SPRING THROUGH THE HOLES AND TWIST THE ENDS ABOUT TO HOLD THE SPRINGS IN PLACE.

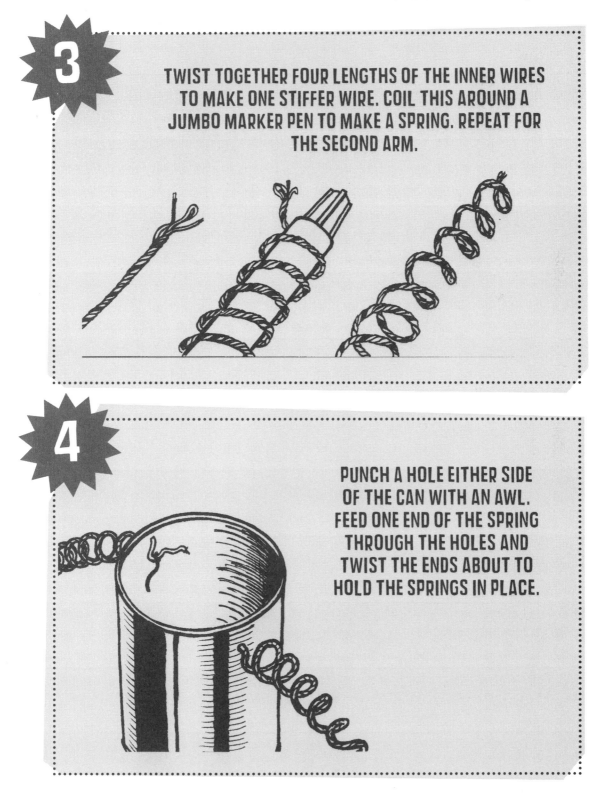

5

IN THE BOTTOM OF THE CAN, PUNCH HOLES AS SHOWN. FIX THE TOPS OF THE 'LEG' SPRINGS WITH BITS OF WIRE LOOPED OVER THE SPRING, FEED THROUGH THE HOLES AND TWIST TOGETHER USING PLIERS. (DON'T TWIST TOO MUCH OR THEY SNAP!)

6

FIX THE LEG SPRINGS TO THE BLOCK OF WOOD WITH U-NAILS. THEN GLUE THE PLASTIC DOME TO THE LID OF THE CAN AND PUT THE LID ON.

7

IF YOU HAVE A LITTLE WIND-UP TOY, LIKE OUR CHATTERING TEETH, WIND IT UP AND POP IT INSIDE THE CAN – THEN WATCH MISTER WIBBLE WOBBLE!

PROJECT 16:
LARRY THE LAMP

BE LIGHT YEARS AHEAD WITH THIS ROBOT LAMP! WE MADE THIS USING THE FITTINGS FROM AN OLD LAMP WE FOUND IN A JUNK SHOP. THE LAMP SHADE WAS TURNED INTO THE ROBOT'S HEAD USING FABRIC PAINT PENS. THE BODY WAS AN OLD AMARETTI TIN. IF YOU CAN FIND A VINTAGE TIN, OR ONE WITH AN OLD-FASHIONED DESIGN, THERE'S NO NEED TO PAINT OVER IT. IT WILL LOOK COOL LEFT AS IT IS. THE ARMS AND LEGS WERE OLD ELECTRIC PLUGS WITH PART OF THE CABLE LEFT ATTACHED. WE USED PLASTIC PLUMBING PIPE AND CONNECTORS FOR LEGS AND FEET. YOU'LL NEED DAD TO HELP WITH THE ELECTRICAL WORKINGS TO BE SURE THE LAMP IS SAFE.

HE WILL NEED: WIRE STRIPPERS / CUTTERS, DRILL, HACKSAW, SCREWDRIVERS (TO REMOVE AND REPLACE THE LAMP PLUG), STRONG GLUE.

1

WE DRILLED A HOLE NEAR THE TOP OF EACH SIDE OF THE TIN, CUT THE OLD PLUG CABLES TO LENGTH AND FED THEM THROUGH THE HOLES – THEN KNOTTED THEM SO THEY STAYED IN PLACE.

2

NEXT WE DRILLED A HOLE IN THE BACK OF THE TIN (NEAR THE BOTTOM) AND ONE IN THE CENTRE OF THE LID, TO FEED THE LAMP CABLE THROUGH. YOU NEED TO REMOVE THE PLUG TO DO THIS. USE STRONG GLUE TO SECURE THE LAMP FITTING TO THE TIN LID.

3 THE LEGS AND FEET WERE TWO EQUAL LENGTHS OF PIPE. CUT WITH A HACKSAW, GLUE TO PIPE CONNECTORS AT EACH END, THEN GLUE TO THE BOTTOM OF THE TIN.

4 WHILST THE GLUE DRIED, WE DECORATED THE SHADE WITH OUR FABRIC PENS AND FITTED IT. LASTLY, DAD REFITTED THE PLUG... AND SWITCHED ON!

PROJECT 17: GREETING CARD

TO MAKE THIS SIMPLE POP-UP CARD YOU MAY SCAN AND PRINT OUR DESIGNS OR DRAW YOUR OWN VERSION TO THE SAME DIMENSIONS.

ALL YOU NEED IS THREE SHEETS OF A4 CARD OR THICK PAPER, SCISSORS AND SOME PAPER GLUE.

THIS IS THE IMAGE THAT WILL POP UP INSIDE THE CARD.
OPPOSITE IS THE FRONT OF THE CARD.

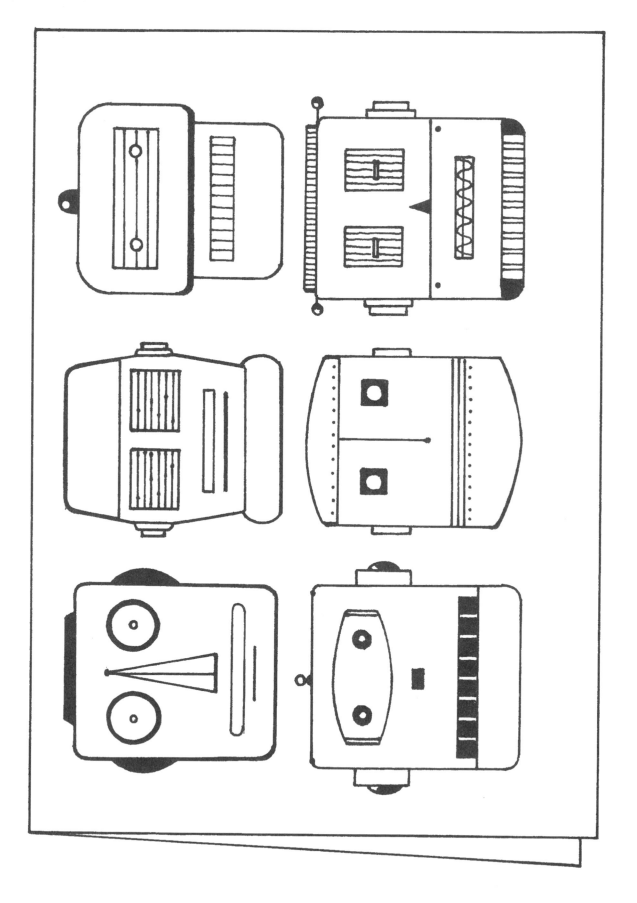

1

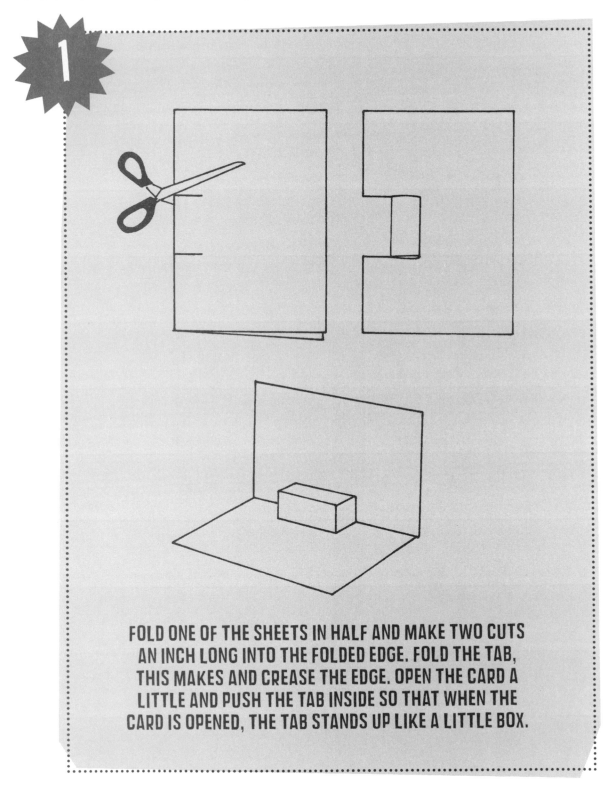

FOLD ONE OF THE SHEETS IN HALF AND MAKE TWO CUTS
AN INCH LONG INTO THE FOLDED EDGE. FOLD THE TAB,
THIS MAKES AND CREASE THE EDGE. OPEN THE CARD A
LITTLE AND PUSH THE TAB INSIDE SO THAT WHEN THE
CARD IS OPENED, THE TAB STANDS UP LIKE A LITTLE BOX.

2

FOLD A SECOND SHEET OF CARD IN HALF AND GLUE THE FIRST INSIDE IT.

3

THE THIRD SHEET IS FOR YOUR POP-UP IMAGE. COLOUR AND CUT IT OUT AND GLUE IT TO THE FRONT OF THE TAB.

4

NOW ALL YOU NEED TO DO IS DECIDE WHO YOU ARE GOING TO SEND IT TO!

HAPPY BIRTHDAY TO DAD
LOVE OTTO (& SCOOTER!) X

PROJECT 18: *DOOR STORE*

HERE'S A HELPFUL ROBOT WHO NOT ONLY LOOKS COOL BUT KEEPS YOUR ROOM TIDY BY STORING STUFF IN HIS POCKETS. IT'S MADE BY STITCHING FELT TOGETHER. DON'T WORRY IF YOU'RE NOT GREAT AT SEWING (WE'RE NOT!) – BIG STITCHES WORK FINE. TRY USING COTTON IN COLOURS THAT CONTRAST WITH THE FELT. CHECK OUT OUR DIAGRAM OF SUGGESTED MEASUREMENTS TO WORK OUT HOW MUCH FELT YOU'LL NEED. THE DETAILS CAN BE MADE FROM ODD SCRAPS.

YOU'LL NEED: SCISSORS AND/OR A CRAFT KNIFE THREE LENGTHS OF WOODEN DOWELLING, A BIG SEWING NEEDLE AND THICK COLOURED COTTON, TWO SCREW-IN HOOKS.

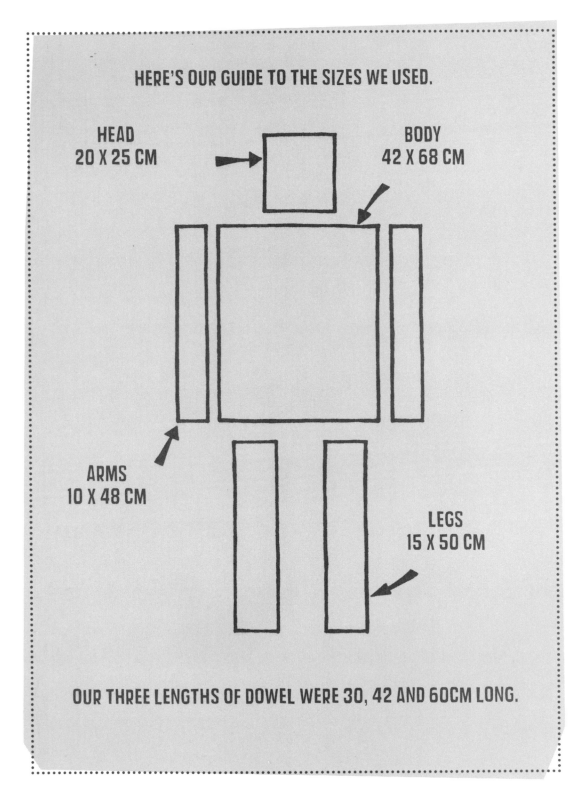

HERE'S OUR GUIDE TO THE SIZES WE USED.

HEAD
20 X 25 CM

BODY
42 X 68 CM

ARMS
10 X 48 CM

LEGS
15 X 50 CM

OUR THREE LENGTHS OF DOWEL WERE 30, 42 AND 60CM LONG.

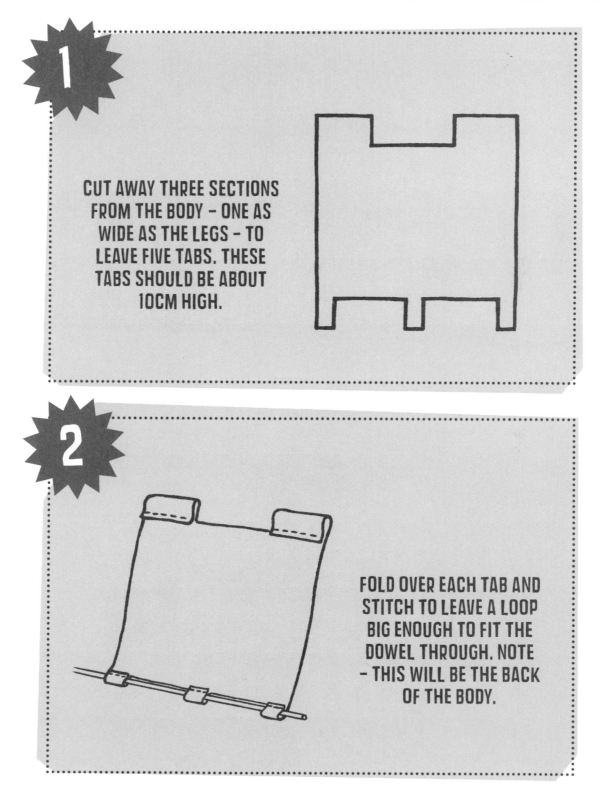

1

CUT AWAY THREE SECTIONS FROM THE BODY – ONE AS WIDE AS THE LEGS – TO LEAVE FIVE TABS. THESE TABS SHOULD BE ABOUT 10CM HIGH.

2

FOLD OVER EACH TAB AND STITCH TO LEAVE A LOOP BIG ENOUGH TO FIT THE DOWEL THROUGH. NOTE – THIS WILL BE THE BACK OF THE BODY.

3

DO THE SAME TO THE TOP AND BOTTOM OF THE HEAD.

AND TO THE TOP OF EACH ARM AND LEG.

4

CUT OUT THREE CIRCLES OF EQUAL SIZE (TRY CUTTING ROUND A PLATE WITH A CRAFT KNIFE FOR A NEAT RESULT). CUT ONE OF THE CIRCLES IN HALF. MAKE ROUND POCKETS BY SEWING EACH SEMI-CIRCLE TO A CIRCLE.

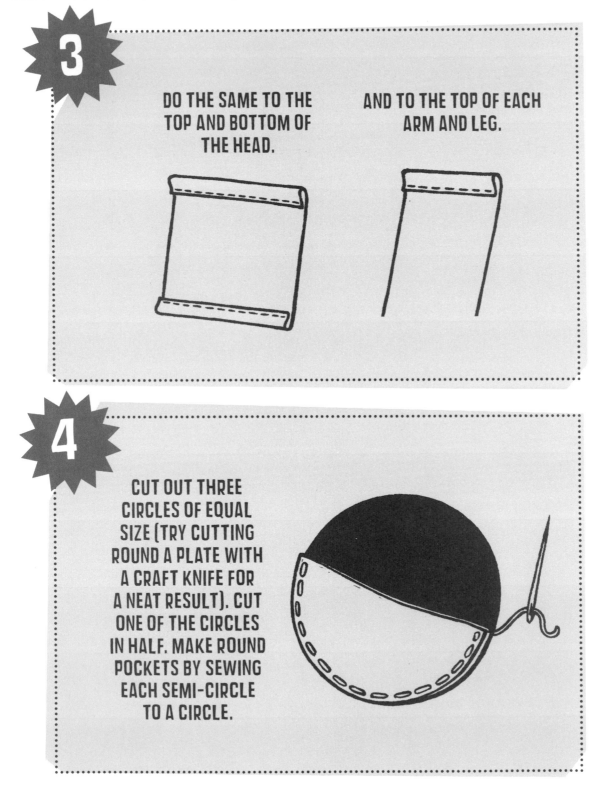

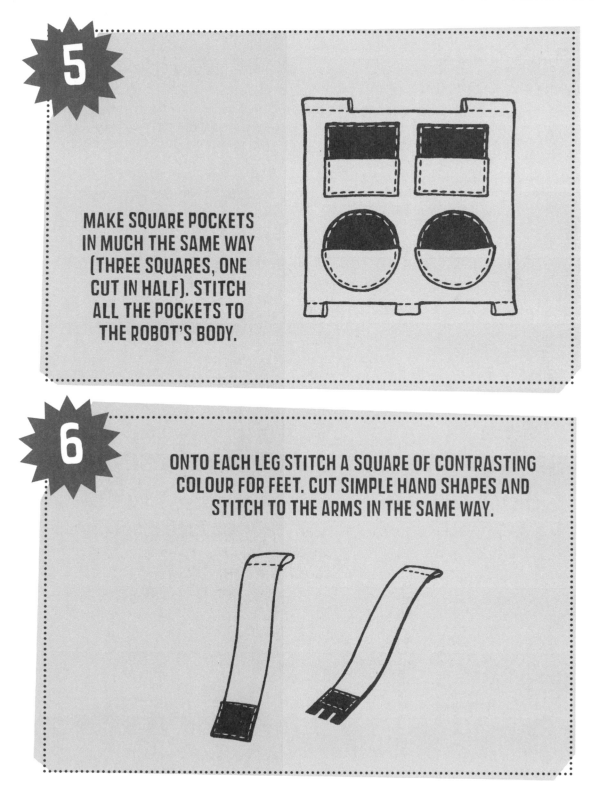

5

MAKE SQUARE POCKETS IN MUCH THE SAME WAY (THREE SQUARES, ONE CUT IN HALF). STITCH ALL THE POCKETS TO THE ROBOT'S BODY.

6

ONTO EACH LEG STITCH A SQUARE OF CONTRASTING COLOUR FOR FEET. CUT SIMPLE HAND SHAPES AND STITCH TO THE ARMS IN THE SAME WAY.

7

CUT SIMPLE SHAPES FOR THE EYES AND MOUTH. OUR EYES WERE MADE BY STICKING ONE CIRCLE TO ANOTHER SLIGHTLY LARGER ONE. IF THESE BITS ARE TOO TRICKY TO SEW, TRY USING FABRIC GLUE.

8

NOW CONSTRUCT THE ROBOT BY FEEDING THE LENGTHS OF DOWEL THROUGH THE LOOPS.

9

FINALLY, GET DAD TO SCREW THE TWO HOOKS INTO THE DOOR. HANG UP THE ROBOT BY THE HEAD DOWEL, AND STORE WHAT YOU LIKE IN THE POCKETS.

PROJECT 19:
ROBO PIRATE

GENERALLY, ROBOTS ARE DESIGNED TO BE HELPFUL AND SERVE HUMANS, BUT WHAT HAPPENS IF THEY GO WRONG? THIS FELLOW HAS MALFUNCTIONED AND IS INTENT ON NOTHING BUT MISCHIEF! YOU'D BETTER HIDE YOUR PIECES OF EIGHT.

HE IS MADE FROM A CARDBOARD CARTON, TWO TUNA CANS AND TWO CARDBOARD TUBES, ONE THINNER THAN THE OTHER, BUT THE SAME LENGTH. YOU'LL ALSO NEED: SHEET OF METALLIC SILVER CARD, STICK-ON HOOK, SHEET OF WHITE PAPER OR CARD. WE USED ALL-PURPOSE GLUE, SCISSORS AND TAPE.

1

GLUE THE TWO CANS TOGETHER AND STICK THEM TO THE TOP OF THE BOX. THEN TAPE THE TUBES TO THE BOTTOM. WE PAINTED THE WIDER TUBE BLACK AND THE THINNER ONE BROWN WITH A WOOD GRAIN EFFECT DRAWN ON IN BLACK INK.

2

CUT OUT THE CUTLASS SHAPE FROM THE SILVER CARD. TURN IT OVER AND DRAW ROUND IT TO CUT OUT THE SAME SHAPE IN REVERSE. STICK THEM TOGETHER, SILVER SIDE OUT, FOLDING THE TWO TABS TO MAKE A FLAT SURFACE FOR STICKING.

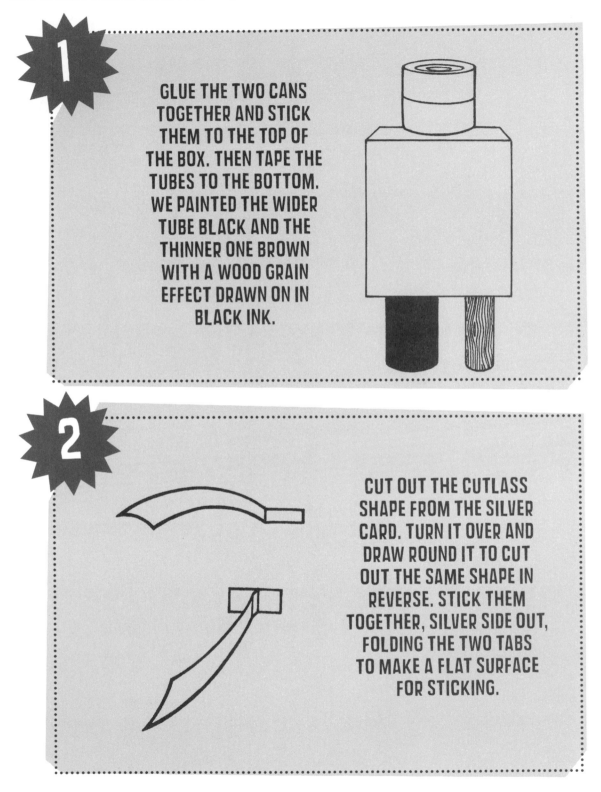

3

CUT A PIECE OF WHITE PAPER TO SIZE TO STICK ROUND THE CANS. IT'S EASIEST TO DRAW THE FACE ON BEFORE YOU STICK ON THE PAPER.

4

LASTLY, DECORATE THE BODY, STICK ON THE CUTLASS AND HOOK AND PREPARE TO WALK THE PLANK!

128

PROJECT 20:
ROBO SANTA

HOW DOES SANTA CLAUS FIND THE TIME TO MAKE PRESENTS FOR EVERY GIRL AND BOY ON THE PLANET AND DELIVER THEM ALL IN ONE NIGHT? IF YOU'VE EVER ASKED A GROWN-UP HUMAN, THEY PROBABLY TOLD YOU HE DOES IT WITH THE HELP OF HIS MANY ELVES. THIS, OF COURSE, IS NONSENSE! SANTA'S LAPLAND FACTORY IS A FULLY AUTOMATED 21ST CENTURY OPERATION RUN ENTIRELY BY ROBOTS.

WE MADE TWO ROBO-SANTAS, ONE TO DECORATE THE CHRISTMAS TABLE, THE OTHER, A LIFE-SIZE ROBO-SANTA, TO STAND ON THE LAWN (BY THE WAY – THE BIT ABOUT THE REINDEER IS TRUE).

TO MAKE THE 'TABLE' SANTA FOLLOW THE SAME INSTRUCTIONS FOR OUR 'CARDBOARD CLASSIC' BUT DECORATE IT LIKE THIS. WE TRIMMED IT WITH COTTON WOOL.

OUR OUTDOOR ROBO-SANTA WAS BUILT IN MUCH THE SAME WAY BUT USING MUCH BIGGER BOXES AND CARDBOARD TUBING. IT WAS WELL COVERED WITH PAPER MACHE, PAINTED THEN VARNISHED ALL OVER TO WATER PROOF. THE BODY HAS CUT-AWAY SECTIONS AND IS FILLED WITH <u>OUTDOOR</u> FLASHING LIGHTS. THE TRIM IS THICK WHITE TINSEL AND THE SANTA HAT, FROM A GIFT STORE.

ROBOT LIBRARY

ZIPPY, AS YOU CAN SEE, IS QUITE THE ARTIST!
ON THE FOLLOWING PAGES HE'S DRAWN SOME
DETAILS TO HELP YOU DECORATE YOUR ROBOTS.
THERE ARE EYES, MOUTHS, DIALS AND GAUGES.
SCAN AND PRINT OR PHOTOCOPY THEM,
THEN COLOUR THEM IN, CUT THEM OUT
AND STICK THEM ON! VOILA!

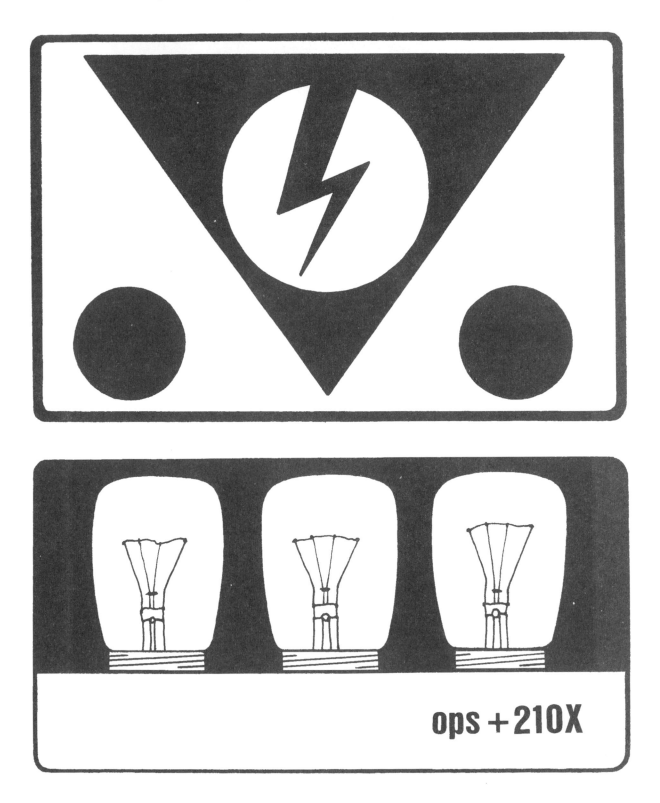

ops + 210X

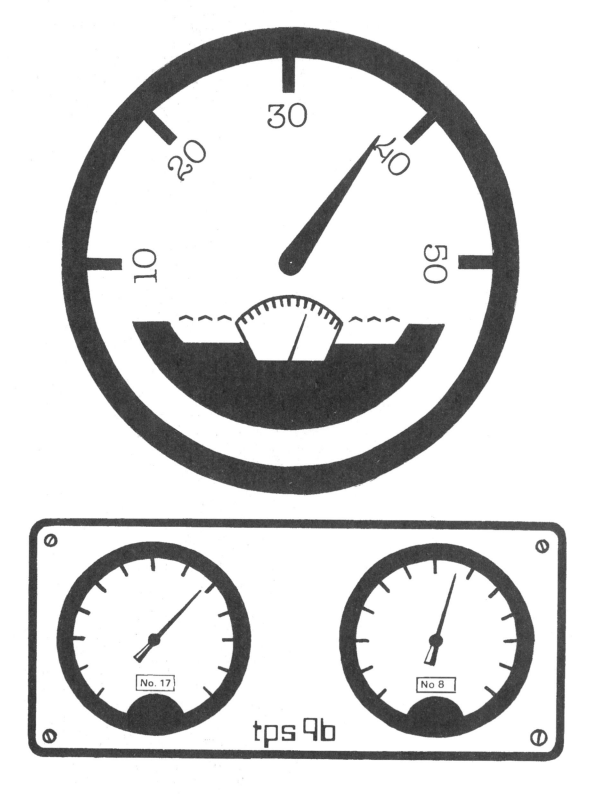

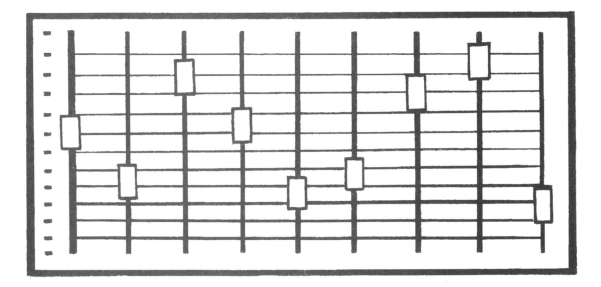

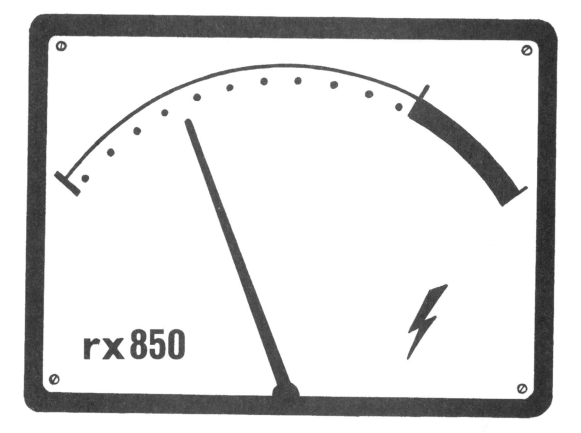

rx850

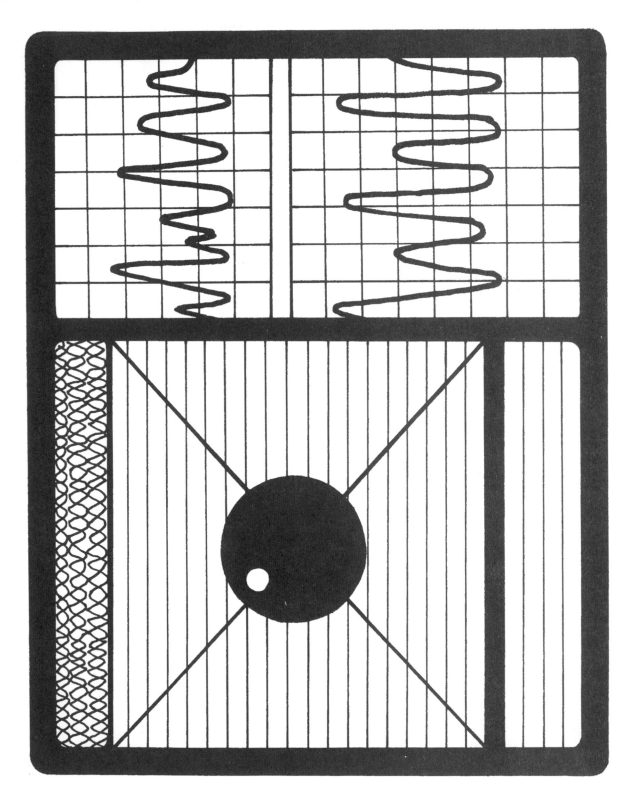

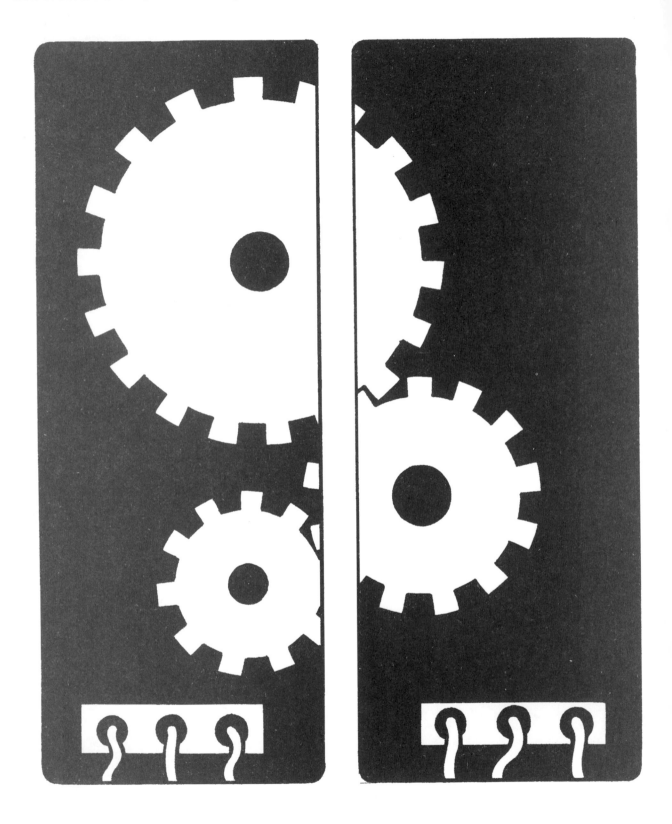

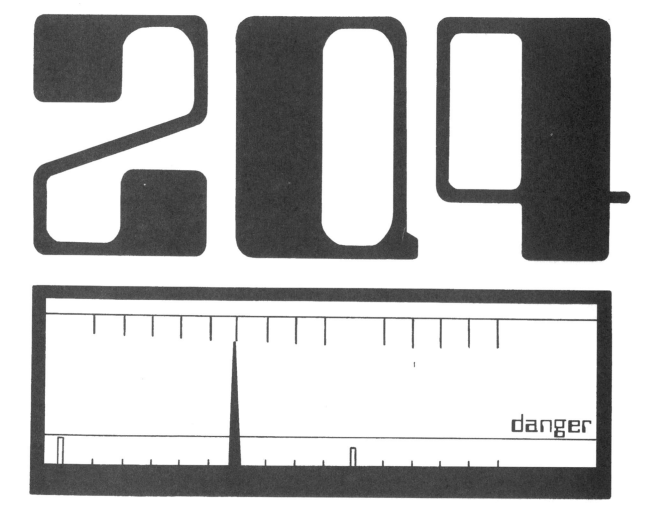

danger

TWIKI

TWIKI (PRONOUNCED TWEE-KEE) IS A LITTLE ROBOT, JUST A METRE HIGH, BUT HE HAS A BIG PERSONALITY. HE WAS BUCK ROGERS' SIDEKICK IN THE TV SERIES BUCK ROGERS IN THE 25TH CENTURY AND WAS PLAYED BETWEEN 1979 AND 1981 BY FELIX SILLA. HIS CHARACTER WAS VOICED BY BOB ELYEA AND MEL BLANC (WHO WAS THE VOICE OF BUGS BUNNY, DAFFY DUCK, SYLVESTER THE CAT AND LOTS MORE OF MY FAVOURITE CARTOON CHARACTERS).

HE WAS ACTUALLY BUILT TO WORK IN SPACE MINES AND HIS MODEL NUMBER WAS TWKE-4, BUT TWIKI IS A BIT EASIER TO SAY. IN SOME EPISODES TWIKI HAS A COMPUTER NAMED DR. THEOPOLIS WHICH HE WEARS ROUND HIS NECK LIKE A BIG MEDAL. HE IS BEST REMEMBERED FOR HIS CATCHPHRASE, 'BIDI-BIDI-BIDI'.

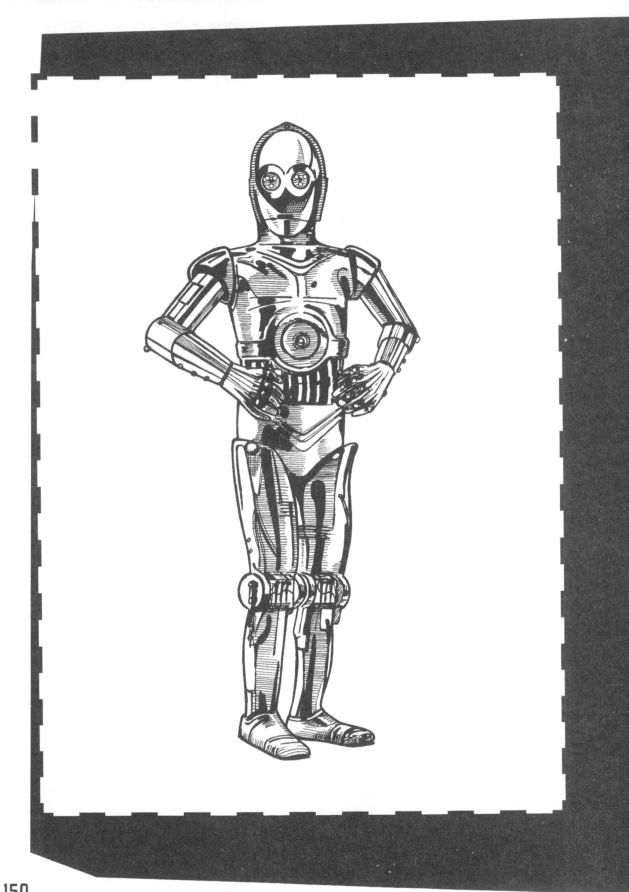

C3PO

ASK ANY ROBOT WHAT HIS FAVOURITE FILM IS, HE'LL PROBABLY SAY STAR WARS. THERE ARE SIX STAR WARS FILMS AND C3PO APPEARS IN ALL OF THEM, PLAYED BY ANTHONY DANIELS.

HE IS A PROTOCOL DROID DESIGNED TO SERVE HUMANS, HE CLAIMS TO BE FLUENT IN OVER SIX MILLION FORMS OF COMMUNICATION, WHICH IS ABOUT SIX MILLION MORE THAN ME! HIS JOB AS A PROTOCOL DROID IS TO HELP WITH PROBLEMS OF ETIQUETTE, CUSTOM AND TRANSLATION BETWEEN FOREIGN CULTURES. THIS IS VERY USEFUL IN SPACE, WHERE THERE ARE ALIEN CREATURES EVEN WEIRDER THAN YOU HUMANS!

C3PO IS USUALLY SEEN WITH HIS OLD PAL R2-D2. THREEPIO HAS THE SINGULAR HONOUR OF BEING THE CHARACTER TO UTTER THE FIRST LINE IN THE FIRST STAR WARS FILM, IN 1977 AND THE LAST LINE IN THE FINAL FILM, REVENGE OF THE SITH, IN 2005.

THE DALEKS

THE DALEKS ARE THE SCARIEST OF ALL ROBOTS. BUT THEY'RE NOT REALLY ROBOTS! THEY ARE A SPECIES OF EXTRA-TERRESTRIAL CYBERNETIC ORGANISMS. TRY SAYING THAT WHEN YOU HAVEN'T BEEN OILED! THEY FEATURE IN THE LONG-RUNNING BRITISH TV SERIES DOCTOR WHO. DALEKS WERE ORIGINALLY CREATED BY THE MAD SCIENTIST DAVROS ON THE PLANET SKARO DURING THE FINAL YEARS OF A THOUSAND-YEAR-LONG WAR BETWEEN THE KALEDS AND THE THALS.

HE EXPERIMENTED WITH LIVING KALED CELLS MUTATED BY THE WAR, TAKING THEIR MUTATED FORM AND PLACING THEM IN A TANK-LIKE MECHANICAL SHELL, COMPLETE WITH LIFE SUPPORT.

THE RESULT WAS THE DALEK – AN ANAGRAM OF KALED – A RACE BENT ON DOMINATING THE UNIVERSE. DOCTOR WHO WAS ON TV WHEN MY DAD WAS QUITE NEW. WHEN THEY APPEARED ON SCREEN HE USED TO HIDE BEHIND THE SOFA!

OTTO'S FAVOURITE ROBOTS 4

K-9

K-9 IS THE NAME OF SEVERAL ROBOTIC 'DOGS' FEATURING IN THE BRITISH TV SERIES DOCTOR WHO. K-9 WAS ALSO IN A NUMBER OF TV SPIN-OFFS: K-9 AND COMPANY, THE SARAH JANE ADVENTURES AND K-9, VOICED MAINLY BY JOHN LEESON AND FOR A FEW EPISODES BY DAVID BRIERLEY.

THERE HAVE BEEN FOUR K-9 UNITS IN ALL. TWO OF THEM APPEARED ALONGSIDE THE DOCTOR, PLAYED BY TOM BAKER – MY DAD SAYS HE WAS THE BEST!

HE ASSISTED THE DOCTOR WITH A LASER WEAPON CONCEALED IN HIS NOSE! K-9 HAD A VAST COMPUTER INTELLIGENCE AND AN ENCYCLOPAEDIC KNOWLEDGE. HE IS MOST FAMOUS FOR HIS CATCHPHRASE 'AFFIRMATIVE', WHICH IS A FANCY WORD FOR YES. I THINK MY DOG SCOOTER IS A BIT LIKE K-9 WITHOUT THE VAST INTELLIGENCE.

KITT

KITT IS THE SHORTENED NAME FOR A SUPERCOMPUTER SYSTEM (KNIGHT INDUSTRIES TWO THOUSAND) INSTALLED IN A 1982 PONTIAC TRANS-AM SPORTS CAR. KITT IS DRIVEN BY MICHAEL KNIGHT (PLAYED BY DAVID HASSELHOFF) IN THE TV SERIES KNIGHT RIDER. THE CAR HAS LOTS OF SPECIAL FEATURES INCLUDING A MICROPROCESSOR WHICH ALLOWS KITT TO THINK, LEARN AND COMMUNICATE.

HE HAS A SPECIALLY ARMOURED BODY WHICH RESISTS EXPLOSIVES – BULLETS JUST BOUNCE OFF! HE EVEN HAS X-RAY VISION! ALL THIS TECHNOLOGY ALLOWS HIM TO HELP MICHAEL FIGHT CRIME AND INJUSTICE. IN A 21ST-CENTURY VERSION OF KNIGHT RIDER, KITT STOOD FOR KNIGHT INDUSTRIES THREE THOUSAND AND WAS 'PLAYED' BY A FORD MUSTANG SHELBY GT500KR. THE KITT IN MY PICTURE IS THE ORIGINAL PONTIAC, WHICH IS STILL MY FAVOURITE.

MARVIN THE PARANOID ANDROID

MARVIN IS FROM DOUGLAS ADAMS' THE HITCH-HIKERS GUIDE TO THE GALAXY. HE SERVES ON THE STARSHIP HEART OF GOLD AND WAS BUILT BY THE SIRIUS CYBERNETICS CORPORATION.

HE CLAIMS TO BE 50,000 TIMES MORE INTELLIGENT THAN THE AVERAGE HUMAN, SO HIS BORING TASKS ON THE STARSHIP, LIKE CHECKING THE AIRLOCKS AND TIDYING UP, DO NOT ENGAGE THE TINIEST FRACTION OF HIS BRAIN.

AS A RESULT, MARVIN IS BORED AND DEPRESSED AND SPENDS MOST OF HIS TIME GRUMBLING. IF I TOLD HIM HE WAS IN MY LIST OF FAVOURITE ROBOTS, HE'D PROBABLY SAY, ' FAVOURITE? ME? YOU'RE TRYING TO BE NICE AREN'T YOU? IT'S NO USE YOU KNOW. OH DEAR...'

METAL MICKEY

METAL MICKEY FIRST APPEARED ON A BRITISH CHILDREN'S TV SHOW CALLED THE SATURDAY BANANA! HE MUST HAVE BEEN A HIT BECAUSE HE SOON WENT ON TO STAR IN HIS OWN SITCOM, THE METAL MICKEY TV SHOW. MICKEY WAS CREATED, CONTROLLED AND VOICED BY JOHNNY EDWARD AS A MODERNIZED VERSION OF A 1950S SPACE TOY.

IN THE SITCOM, MICKEY WAS DESIGNED BY THE YOUNGEST CHILD OF A TYPICAL BRITISH FAMILY, KEN, TO DO ALL THE BORING HOUSEHOLD CHORES THAT KEN DIDN'T WANT TO DO. BUT HE USUALLY ENDED UP ATTRACTING TROUBLE RATHER THAN HELPING – NOT LIKE ME AT ALL! LUCKILY, MICKEY POSSESSED MAGIC POWERS THAT ALLOWED HIM TO TRAVEL IN TIME, FIGHT OFF ALIENS AND AVERT DISASTERS. HE LIKED TO EAT SOMETHING CALLED ATOMIC THUNDERBUSTERS AND HAD A FAMOUS CATCHPHRASE – 'BOOGIE BOOGIE'.

OTTO'S FAVOURITE ROBOTS 8

R2-D2

HERE'S ANOTHER FROM MY FAVOURITE FILM SERIES, STAR WARS. IT IS C3PO'S LITTLE SIDEKICK R2-D2. 'ARTOO' IS AN ASTROMECH DROID WHO, LIKE THREEPIO, APPEARS IN ALL SIX STAR WARS FILMS, PLAYED BY KENNY BAKER. ARTOO AND THREEPIO FIRST MEET IN EPISODE 1: A PHANTOM MENACE, WHEN ARTOO FOLLOWS OBI-WAN KENOBI TO TATOOINE.

IN EPISODE III, C3PO HAS HIS MEMORY WIPED TO PROTECT THE IDENTITIES AND LOCATION OF LUKE SKYWALKER AND PRINCESS LEIA ORGANA, AND R2-D2 BECOMES THE ONLY CHARACTER WHO KNOWS THE FULL HISTORY OF THE SKYWALKER FAMILY. WHEN MY DAD WATCHED THE FILMS WITH ME, HE SAID ARTOO LOOKED A LITTLE LIKE OUR DUSTBIN. I DON'T THINK OUR DUSTBIN IS NEARLY AS COOL.

OTTO'S FAVOURITE ROBOTS **9**

ROBBY THE ROBOT

ROBBY THE ROBOT HAS HAD ONE OF THE LONGEST CAREERS OF ALL ROBOT STARS. HE FIRST APPEARED IN THE FILM FORBIDDEN PLANET WAY BACK IN 1956. THAT'S BEFORE MY DAD WAS EVEN BUILT! FOR A WHILE, ROBBY WAS THE MOST FAMOUS ROBOT ON EARTH, APPEARING IN SEVERAL SCIENCE FICTION FILMS AND TV SHOWS.

HE WAS STILL WORKING AS RECENTLY AS 2005, WHEN HE APPEARED IN A TV SHOW CALLED STACKED. HE IS CERTAINLY THE TALLEST OF MY FAVOURITE ROBOTS, MEASURING SEVEN FEET, AND I THINK HE LOOKS PRETTY SCARY. BUT, IN FACT, HE'S RATHER NICE. ROBBY WAS PROGRAMMED BY DR MORBIUS IN FORBIDDEN PLANET TO BE HELPFUL. I THINK I'D LIKE TO BE LIKE ROBBY WHEN I GROW UP, BUT DAD SAYS IT'S UNLIKELY I'LL REACH SEVEN FEET.

OTTO'S FAVOURITE ROBOTS
THE TIN MAN

THE TIN MAN, OR, MORE CORRECTLY, THE TIN WOODMAN, IS VERY FAMOUS. YOU'LL HAVE SEEN HIM IN THE FILM THE WIZARD OF OZ. IT WAS MADE IN 1939, BUT THE TIN MAN FIRST APPEARED IN A CHILDREN'S BOOK, THE WONDERFUL WIZARD OF OZ, IN 1900 – THAT'S BEFORE THE WORD ROBOT WAS EVEN INVENTED!

IN THE ORIGINAL STORY THE TIN WOODMAN ACTUALLY STARTS LIFE AS A MUNCHKIN NAMED NICK CHOPPER. THE WICKED WITCH OF THE EAST PUTS A SPELL ON HIS AXE TO MAKE IT CHOP HIM TO PIECES! BUT NICK REPLACES ALL HIS PARTS WITH TIN ONES UNTIL, EVENTUALLY, HE IS MADE COMPLETELY OF TIN. I'M GLAD THAT'S NOT HOW I CAME TO BE MADE OF METAL! THE POOR OLD TIN MAN GOES RUSTY IN A STORM AND IS STUCK UNTIL DOROTHY AND THE SCARECROW FIND HIM. I'M SURE YOU KNOW WHAT HAPPENS AFTER THAT!